THE

FORM OF GOVERNMENT

AND

THE DISCIPLINE

OF THE

United Presbyterian Church

OF

NORTH AMERICA.

PHILADELPHIA:
WM. S. YOUNG—1023 RACE STREET.
1860.

EXTRACT

FROM THE MINUTES OF THE GENERAL ASSEMBLY OF THE UNITED PRESBYTERIAN CHURCH, MET IN PHILADELPHIA, MAY 23D, 1860.

Resolved, That the Book of Discipline submitted by the Committee appointed by the last Assembly, and which has been under the consideration of this Assembly, be overtured to the Presbyteries for their consideration, and that they be instructed to report their judgment thereon to the next General Assembly.

JOSEPH CLOKEY, *Moderator*.
JAMES PRESTLEY, *Prin. Clerk*.

OF GOVERNMENT.

CHAPTER I.

GENERAL PRINCIPLES.

SECTION 1. "God alone is Lord of the conscience, and has left it free from the doctrines and commandments of men, which are in anything contrary to his word, or beside it, in matters of faith or worship." It is, therefore, an inalienable right common to all men, to worship God according to his word: and no earthly power can justly deprive them of the right to worship God according to the dictates of their own consciences, unless its exercise infringes upon the rights of others.

2. In harmony with the above principle of common right, we affirm, that every Christian church, or association of particular churches, has an unquestionable right to settle and declare the terms of admission into

its fellowship, the qualifications of its ministers and members, and the whole system of its internal polity and government, according to its own views of what Christ hath in these respects appointed. In doing this she may err, in the sight of the church's Head, to whom alone she is accountable, yet does not thereby infringe upon the liberty or the rights of others.

3. The Word of God is the only rule of faith and practice, and whatever cannot be established from this word, can have no authority to bind the conscience. "To the law and to the testimony, if they speak not according to this word, it is because there is no light in them." All the terms of the church's fellowship must then be drawn from the written word, and be such as can be defended by an appeal to its authority, either express or necessarily inferential.

4. The terms of the church's fellowship should include both faith and practice. An unscriptural belief as really sets the authority of God's word at defiance as an unholy practice. The tendency of the truth is to promote holiness; as our Saviour says, "Sanctify them through thy truth." The church should, therefore, take order that her teachers, other officers and members, be sound in the faith and holy in their lives.

5. Although the authority to judge, as ne-

cessity requires in the present state, be lodged with fallible men, yet being the ministerial exercise of Christ's own authority, it should be submitted to, as far as it is exercised according to the law of his house, laid down in the holy Scriptures. "He that heareth you heareth me." "Whatsoever ye shall bind on earth shall be bound in heaven; and whatsoever ye shall loose on earth, shall be loosed in heaven."

6. As the kingdom of Christ is not of this world, and the discipline of his house is purely moral or spiritual, not attended with any civil or penal effects on the bodies or estates of men, but designed to reach their consciences, its efficacy must depend on its own justice, and the approbation and blessing of the great Head of the Church.

7. That all things may "be done to edifying," and "decently and in order," it is the right and duty of the church to establish and ordain such forms and rules of procedure, as prudence and experience may show to be necessary, for the speedy and orderly transaction of all business in her various assemblies.

CHAPTER II.

OF THE CHURCH.

SECTION 1. There is one universal, visible church, 1 Cor. xii. 12, 13, which consists of all those persons, in every nation, who profess the true religion of Christ, and obedience to his laws, together with their children. Rev. v. 9; Acts ii. 38, 39, 41; 1 Cor. i. 2; 2 Cor. ix. 13.

2. This church is Christ's kingdom in the world. Psal. ii. 6; Dan. vii. 14; Eph. i. 22, 23. It is spiritual, free and independent, subject only to his law, and to be governed exclusively by officers of his appointment.

3. As the whole multitude constituting the visible church cannot meet in one place, it is reasonable, and warranted by Scripture example, that they should be divided into many particular churches or congregations. Gal. i. 21, 22; Rev. i. 4, 20; ii. 1.

4. A particular church consists of a number of professing Christians, with their children, voluntarily associated together, for the purpose of observing and enjoying divine ordinances, and submitting themselves to the laws of Christ's house. Acts ii. 41, 47; 1 Cor. vii. 14; Acts ii. 39; Mark x. 14.

5. The Lord Jesus has appointed officers, ordinances and a government in his church.

CHAPTER III.

OF THE OFFICERS OF THE CHURCH.

ARTICLE I.

DIFFERENT KINDS OF OFFICERS.

SECTION 1. At the first establishment of the New Testament Church, our Lord appointed some extraordinary officers, such as apostles and prophets, endued with miraculous gifts, all of which were temporary, and have ceased. Matt. x. 1, 8; Eph. iv. 11.

2. The ordinary and perpetual officers of the church, are Bishops or Presbyters, 1 Tim. iii. 1; Eph. iv. 11, 12, ruling elders, 1 Tim. v. 17, and deacons. Phil. i. 1.

ARTICLE II.

OF BISHOPS OR PASTORS.

The pastor or teaching elder is the highest ordinary officer in the Christian Church. Various names are given to him in Scripture, each expressive of something conspicuous in his official relations and duties. Thus, he is called the "angel of the church," Rev. ii. 1; i. 20; iii. 1, 7; Mal. ii. 7; "bishop" or "overseer," Acts xx. 28; "pastor," Jer. iii. 15; 1 Pet. v. 2, 3, 4; "minister," 1 Cor. iv. 1; 2 Cor. iii. 6; "presbyter" or "elder," 1 Pet. v. 1; Tit. i. 5; 1 Tim. v. 1, 17, 19; an ambassador. 2 Cor. v. 20; Eph. vi. 20.

ARTICLE III.

OF RULING ELDERS.

The ruling elder, as the name imports, is to exercise authority and government in the church, in conjunction with the pastor, and is, in this respect, his equal. He is of the class denominated, in Scripture, "governments," and who are said to "rule well," but to whom it does not belong to labor in word and doctrine. 1 Tim. v. 17; Rom. xii. 7, 8; 1 Cor. xii. 28.

ARTICLE IV.

OF DEACONS.

The deacon, as a distinct officer of the church, is clearly pointed out by the Scriptures. Phil. i. 1; 1 Tim. iii. 8—15. His business is to take care of the poor, and distribute among them the collections raised for their use. Acts vi. 1, 2. To him may also properly be committed the management of all the temporalities of the church. Acts vi. 3, 5, 6.

CHAPTER IV.

OF THE ORDINANCES OF A PARTICULAR CHURCH.

THE ordinances which Christ, the Head, has appointed to be observed in every particular church, are prayer, Acts vi. 4; 1 Tim. ii. 1, praise, Ps. cxlix. 1—9, 11, Col. iii. 16; reading, Acts xv. 21; Luke iv. 16, 17, expounding and preaching the word, Tit. i. 9; Acts x. 42; xxviii. 23; Luke xxiv. 47; 2 Tim. iv. 2, including catechising and teaching from house to house, Heb. v. 12; vi. 1, 2; 1 Cor. iii. 1, 2, administering the sacraments of baptism and the Lord's supper, Matt. xxviii. 19, 20; 1 Cor. xi. 23—26; Mark xvi. 15, 16, public solemn fasting and thanksgiving, Luke v. 35; Ps. l. 14; Phil. iv. 6; Ezra viii. 21, public vowing or covenanting, Ps. lxxvi. 11; Neh. viii., ix., x. chaps.; 2 Cor. v. 5; Isaiah xix. 21; xliv. 5, making collections for the poor and for other pious uses, 1 Cor. xvi. 1—4; Gal. ii. 10, exercising discipline, Heb. xiii. 17; 1 Thess. v. 12, 13, and blessing the people, 2 Cor. xiii. 14; Eph. i. 2; Deut. x. 8.

CHAPTER V.

OF THE GOVERNMENT OF THE CHURCH AND THE VARIOUS JUDICATORIES THEREOF.

SECTION 1. The government of the church must needs be exercised under some certain definite form. This the Lord Jesus Christ, the King and Head of the Church, has not left to be modelled according to the will of men or the maxims of the world, but has Himself instituted one unchangeable form of government. Ezek. xliii. 11, 12.

2. This form of government is Presbyterial, involving in it, as belonging to its essential attributes, representation of the peo-

ple by their rulers, and equality among these, as rulers. 1 Peter v. 4.

3. It is lawful, and agreeable to the word of God, and the practice of the primitive Christians, that the church be governed by congregational, presbyterial, synodical, &c., assemblies, composed of pastors and other elders.

4. The regular subordination of the congregational classis or session to the presbytery; of presbyteries to synod; of synods to a general assembly, is the form of presbyterial church government. This subordination of a part to the whole is rational and Scriptural, and necessary to the unity, peace, and general edification of the whole body. Acts xv. 2, 5, 6.

5. The power which is common to all church assemblies, is that of requiring submission to the laws of Christ's house; and of excluding the disobedient and disorderly from the fellowship of the church. To this end, they have authority to call offenders before them; to cite witnesses who are under their jurisdiction; to hear and determine all such causes and differences as may be brought before them in an orderly manner, and to inflict merited censure upon offenders. Matt. xviii. 15—20; 1 Cor. v. 4, 5.

CHAPTER VI.

OF CHURCH SESSIONS.

SECTION 1. The church session consists of the pastor or pastors, and the ruling elders of a particular congregation. 1 Cor. v. 4.

2. In all ordinary cases, two elders, with the pastor, shall be necessary to constitute a quorum for the transaction of any business.

3. The pastor of the congregation is the standing moderator of the session; but where there is a collegiate charge, either of the pastors may preside, or they may preside alternately, as may be agreed upon by them; and in such case, the other shall be a constituent member of the session.

4. When, for prudential reasons, it may appear advisable that some other minister should preside, the pastor may, with the concurrence of the elders, invite another, being a member of the same presbytery, to preside in that particular case. The same thing may be done in case of the sickness or absence of the pastor.

5. As in all other judicatories of the church, the moderator of the session has a casting vote.

6. It is expedient that there be a minister to act as moderator at every meeting for the exercise of government and discipline. When, therefore, a congregation is vacant, the ses-

sion may either apply to the presbytery to appoint a minister for that purpose, or they may invite one, being a member of the presbytery, to preside on any particular occasion. But where this is impracticable, without great inconvenience, or would occasion such a delay as would be injurious to the interests of religion in the congregation, the elders may, by virtue of their official character and authority, provided there be more than two in the congregation, appoint one of their own number to preside, and then proceed to transact any necessary business.

7. The session may be convened by the pastor when he may judge it requisite, Acts xx. 17; and he shall always convene them when requested to do so by two elders. They may also meet on their own adjournment, and if there be no pastor, by an agreement among the members; and they shall always meet when directed so to do by the presbytery.

8. It is expedient that the congregation be divided by the session into particular districts, to the special superintendence of each of which some particular member shall be assigned.

9. The session is charged with the spiritual government and oversight of the congregation, Heb. xiii. 17; 1 Thes. v. 12, 13; 1 Tim. v. 17. To this end, they have power to inquire into the knowledge, spiritual es-

tate, and conduct of the members of the church, Ezek. xxxiv. 4, to call offenders before them, to summon witnesses, being members of their own congregation, and to introduce, as they may find necessary, other witnesses, when their attendance can be procured; to admonish, to rebuke, to suspend from the sacraments those who are found worthy of censure, 1 Thes. v. 12, 13; 2 Thes. iii. 6, 14, 15, to receive persons into the fellowship of the church, to grant letters of dismission to those who are of good character and standing when applied for, to employ all other scriptural means, competent to their office, for promoting the spiritual interests of the congregation, and to appoint delegates to the higher judicatories of the church.

10. In the admission of members into the church, the session, while taking due care that applicants have competent knowledge of divine truth, and are of blameless life, should imitate the example of our Lord in condescending to the weakness of men. In the case of persons unknown to the session, testimonials of character shall be required, and applicants from other churches shall not be admitted unless it appear that they are acting from a solid conviction of duty, and entertain a spirit of Christian kindness towards the party whose communion is relinquished. Suitable testimonials, if they can

be obtained, should be required in this latter case also, 1 Cor. x. 32; xiv. 33.

11. Testimonials shall at all times be given to members of unexceptionable character, who are about to remove from the congregation, which, if not more than a year old, shall entitle them to communion in sealing ordinances in any congregation under the inspection of the General Assembly.*

12. When members removing to a distance have neglected to apply for testimonials, no subsequent application shall obtain them, unless the session are satisfied that their conversation has been, during their absence, becoming the gospel of Christ.†

13. Testimonials should be signed by order of session, by the minister or clerk of session.

14. Every session shall keep a fair record of their proceedings, which record shall be at least once every year, submitted to the inspection of the presbytery. They shall also keep a fair register of baptisms, of persons admitted to fellowship, and of the deaths and other removals of church members.

CHAPTER VII.

OF THE PRESBYTERY.

SECTION 1. As the church consists of many separate congregations, and these need su-

* See Appendix, No. 1. † See Appendix, No. 2.

pervision, mutual counsel and assistance, in order to maintain soundness of doctrine and regularity of discipline, and to preserve the unity and peace of the whole, by common measures for promoting knowledge and religion, and for preventing infidelity, error, and immorality,* there should be, according to the Scriptures, presbyterial and synodical assemblies. 1 Tim. iv. 14; Acts xv. 2, 3, 4, 6, 22.

2. A presbytery consists of all the ministers and of one ruling elder from each congregation or pastoral charge within a given district.

3. Ministers without charge shall be accounted members of the presbytery within whose bounds they reside, and shall enjoy all the privileges of other members.

4. Though the number of members in a Presbytery cannot be determined by any general rule, yet it is proper that a presbytery consist of not less than two ministers and two ruling elders, and they not connected with the same pastoral charge.

5. Every congregation which has a settled

* The church at Jerusalem consisted of more than one congregation, Acts vi. 1, 6; ix. 31; xxi. 20; ii. 41, 46, 47; iv. 4, and these were under one presbyterial government. Acts xv. 4; xi. 22, 30; xxi. 17, 18; sixth chap. So the church at Ephesus, Acts xix. 18, 19, 20; 1 Cor. xvi. 8, 9, 19, compare with Acts xviii. 19, 24, 26; Acts xx. 17, 18, 25, 28, 30, 31, 36, 37; Rev. ii. 1–6.

pastor or pastors, has a right to be represented by one elder.

6. Where two or more congregations form but one pastoral charge, they shall have but one elder to represent them.

7. Every vacant congregation, or two or more congregations, regularly organized, and able and willing to support a pastor, shall be entitled to be represented by one elder.

8. An elder not known to the presbytery, or to some member thereof, shall produce a certificate of his appointment from the church or churches he represents. Acts xv. 1–6; 1 Cor. xiv. 26, 33, 34.

9. Any two ministers, with as many elders duly appointed as may be present, or any three ministers, being met at the time and place appointed, shall be a quorum competent for the transaction of business. Acts xiv. 26, 27, compare with Acts xi. 18.

11. The presbytery has power to hear and issue complaints and appeals from church sessions, Acts xv. 5, 6, 19, 20, and references for advice or otherwise that come before them in an orderly manner, Acts xviii. 24, 27, compare with Acts xix. 1–7, to examine and license candidates for the holy ministry; 1 Tim. iv. 14; Acts xiii. 2, 3, to ordain, install, remove, and try ministers of the gospel, Acts xv. 28; 1 Cor. v. 3; to examine

and approve or censure the records of church sessions; to resolve questions of doctrine or discipline seriously and reasonably proposed, Acts xv. 10, compare with Gal. ii. 4, 5; to condemn erroneous opinions which injure the purity or peace of the church, Acts xv. 22–24; to visit particular churches, for the purpose of inquiring into their state, and redressing evils which may have arisen in them, Acts xx. 17; vi. 2; xv. 30; to unite and divide congregations, at the request of the people, or to organize new congregations; and, in general, to order whatever belongs to the spiritual welfare and prosperity of the churches under their care. Eph. vi. 18; Phil. iv. 6.

11. As an able, faithful, and godly ministry is of the utmost importance to the church, presbyteries are bound to give diligent attention to training up young men for that office. It belongs to them to examine and admit students of theology, and, in the discharge of this duty, to see that the applicant is of fair moral character, unexceptionable standing as a church member, 1 Tim. iii. 6, manifests an intelligent attachment to the principles of his public profession, gives evidence of a saving acquaintance with divine things, 2 Cor. i. 4, and also that he has made such attainments in literature and science as will fit him to prosecute, with advan-

tage, theological studies, and that he is endowed with such talents and aptness to teach as promise public usefulness.

12. Every student shall be regarded as under the authority of the Presbytery by which he was admitted, until regularly dismissed to the care of another presbytery. Yet this shall not be so understood as to prevent any presbytery, within whose bounds any student may, for the time being, reside, exercising a due supervision and care over him, and if need be reporting any matter in relation to his deportment to his proper presbytery.

13. Presbyteries shall meet at least once in six months, and as much oftener as the necessities of their charge, and the situation of their members will allow.

14. The Presbytery shall meet on its own adjournment; but when an emergency shall require a meeting sooner than the time to which it stands adjourned, the moderator has power to call a meeting. The moderator, or, in case of his absence, death, or inability to act, the stated clerk, shall, with the concurrence, or at the request of two ministers, if there be more than three in the presbytery, if not, of one minister and two elders, the elders being of different congregations, call a special meeting. Care must be taken that sufficient notice be given of the intended

meeting. To this end the moderator or clerk, as the case may be, shall issue a circular letter to each minister and to the session of every vacant congregation, a sufficient time previous to the meeting. This circular shall specify the particular business for which the judicatory is convened, also the time and place of meeting, and nothing else shall be transacted at such meeting, unless, by unanimous consent of the members present, or it have been distinctly stated in the letter that other important business may be transacted.

15. At the opening of every meeting the roll shall be called, and the meeting recorded by the clerk, who shall enter the names of the members present, and also of those who are absent. Reasons for non-attendance at a previous meeting shall be required of absentees.

16. It shall be the duty of the presbytery to keep a fair record of all its proceedings, subject to the inspection of synod; and also to report to synod every year, admissions of students, licensures, ordinations, instalments, receiving and dismissal of members, removal of members by death, the union and division of congregations, and the organization of new ones; and in general whatever important or interesting changes may have taken place within their bounds during the

year. A like report shall also be forwarded to the General Assembly.

17. At every meeting of presbytery a sermon shall be preached, if convenient; and every particular session shall be opened and closed with prayer.

18. Ministers in good standing in other presbyteries, being present, may be invited to sit as corresponding members. Such also may be the case with ministers of sister churches. Such members may deliberate and advise, but shall not vote in any decision of presbytery.

CHAPTER VIII.

OF THE PARTICULAR SYNOD.*

SECTION 1. A synod consists of several presbyteries met together as one body, for the better management of their common concerns. As the presbytery is an assembly of the ministers and of duly commissioned elders, within a given district; so the synod is an assembly of the same, within a larger district including at least three presbyteries; and is in fact only a larger presbytery. The ratio of the representation of elders in the synod shall be the same as in the presbytery.

* It is unnecessary here to repeat the scriptures to which reference has been made under Chapter VII., as they apply equally to a synod as to a presbytery.

2. Any six ministers from two different presbyteries, who shall convene at the time and place appointed, with as many ruling elders as may be present, shall be a quorum for the transaction of business.

3. The synod shall convene at least once every year, meeting on its own adjournment. On a special emergency, it may be convened by the call of the moderator on the application of a presbytery; in this case the call shall be made and the business limited as in a special meeting of presbytery, see Chap. VII., Sec. 14. At the opening of every meeting a sermon shall be delivered by the moderator, or, in case of his absence or inability, by some other member, who shall hold the chair till another moderator be chosen; and every particular session shall be opened and closed with prayer.

4. The same rule, as to the corresponding members, which was laid down with respect to the presbytery, shall apply to the synod.

5. The synod, being immediately superior to the presbytery, has power to hear and issue all appeals regularly brought up from the presbyteries; to hear and issue complaints against the proceedings of presbyteries; to decide on references made to them; to review and censure or approve the records of presbyteries; to redress whatever has been done by presbyteries contrary to order;

to take effectual care that presbyteries act in conformity with the word of God and the standards of the church; to erect new presbyteries, and unite or divide those already erected; to judge in controversies respecting doctrine or discipline; to appoint days of fasting and thanksgiving throughout their bounds; to employ members of presbyteries, or probationers belonging to any of them, in public service; generally to take such order with respect to presbyteries, sessions, and the people under their care, as may, in conformity with the word of God and the established rules of this church, tend to promote the edification, purity, peace, and prosperity of the church; and in fine to propose to the General Assembly for their adoption, such measures as may be for the advantage of the whole church.

6. The synod shall keep a full and fair record of its proceedings, submit them annually to the inspection of the General Assembly, and report to the Assembly the number of its presbyteries, and of their members, and any alterations which have been made in its presbyteries.

CHAPTER IX.

OF THE GENERAL ASSEMBLY.

SECTION 1. The General Assembly is the highest judicatory of the United Presbyterian Church. It shall represent, by presbyterial delegation, all the particular churches, Acts xv. chap. and shall be known by the title of the General Assembly of the United Presbyterian Church of North America.

2. The General Assembly shall consist of an equal delegation of ministers and ruling elders from each presbytery, in the following proportion, viz.: Each presbytery, consisting of not more than seven ministers, shall be entitled to send one minister and one ruling elder; each presbytery consisting of more than seven ministers and not more than fourteen, shall be entitled to send two ministers and two ruling elders; each presbytery consisting of more than fourteen ministers and not more than twenty-one, shall be entitled to send three ministers and three ruling elders; and in a like proportion for any number of ministers beyond twenty-one; and delegates, so appointed, shall be styled Commissioners to the General Assembly.

3. One third of all the delegates, duly commissioned, being assembled at the time and place appointed, shall be a quorum for the transaction of business.

4. The General Assembly shall receive and decide appeals, references, and complaints, regularly brought before them, only on questions of doctrine and the principles of ecclesiastical law, and their decision shall

be an instruction to the court below how to proceed and issue the case. But in no instance shall a case be tried on its merits before the Assembly. They shall review and approve or censure the records of every synod; in all cases submitted to them, in conformity with the standards of the church they shall give their advice and instruction, and they shall constitute the bond of union, peace, concord, and mutual confidence, among all our churches.

5. To the General Assembly also belongs the power of deciding in all controversies respecting doctrine and discipline; of warning or bearing testimony against any error in doctrine or immorality in practice; of erecting new synods when it may be judged necessary; of superintending the general interests of the whole church, of establishing and managing the missionary operations of the church, whether foreign or domestic, of corresponding with other churches in such manner as may be mutually agreed upon; and, in general, of watching over and adopting measures to promote the interest of truth and holiness through all the churches under their care.

6. Before any regulations intended to be permanent and universal shall be adopted and binding on the particular churches, it shall be necessary to transmit them in overture

to all the presbyteries, and to receive the returns of at least a majority of votes of the whole church approving thereof. Such returns of a majority of the presbyteries shall be regarded as authorizing the assembly to enact such regulations, unless peculiar circumstances should, in the view of two-thirds of the whole delegation to the assembly, render it inexpedient.

7. The General Assembly shall meet at least once every year. At the time appointed, the Moderator of the last Assembly, or his alternate, or, in their absence, the oldest minister present, shall open the meeting with a sermon, constitute the assembly, and preside until a new moderator be chosen.

8. Every commissioner to the General Assembly must produce a commission signed by the moderator and clerk of the presbytery by which he is sent; nor can he, without such commission, be entitled to a seat. All commissions shall be examined by the Moderator and Clerk of the last Assembly.*

9. Each session of the Assembly shall be opened and closed with prayer, and when the whole business of the Assembly is finished, and a vote taken to dissolve the present Assembly, the Moderator shall say from the chair, "By virtue of authority to me delegated by the church, I do hereby dissolve this General Assembly, and require another

* For form of commission, see Appendix, No. 10.

General Assembly, chosen in the same manner, to meet at ——— on the —— day of ——— A. D., ——." After which he shall close the sessions by prayer, singing a Psalm, and the Apostolic benediction.

CHAPTER X.

OF THE OFFICERS OF COURTS.

SECTION 1. To the preservation of good order and the despatch of business, it is necessary that there be certain officers in each of the afore mentioned courts, viz.: a Moderator and clerk or clerks.

2. The pastor is the standing Moderator of the session (See Chap. VI., Sec. 3.) The Moderator of the presbytery shall be chosen from year to year, or for a shorter period, as the presbytery may judge best. The Moderator of the synod, and of the General Assembly, shall be chosen at each meeting of those judicatories.

3. The last Moderator, or the member presiding in his place, shall, immediately after constituting the synod or assembly, intimate the election of a new Moderator as the first business. Nominations may then be made in open court, and if more than one member be nominated, the election shall be by ballot.

4. In every judicatory the clerk may be either a member, or some other person, as

shall be deemed expedient. He shall be chosen by an open vote, unless two or more persons be nominated, in which case he shall be chosen by ballot, and his continuance in office shall be during the pleasure of the judicatory.

5. The Moderator possesses, by delegation from the whole body, all authority necessary for the preservation of order, for constituting and adjourning the court, and for directing its operations, according to the rules of the church. He shall state to the judicatory every subject that orderly comes before them, and prevent the introduction of new business at improper seasons. He may propose to the judicatory what appears to him the most regular and speedy way of bringing any business to an issue. He shall prevent members from interrupting one another, except for explanation, and require them, when speaking, to address the chair. He shall prevent speakers from using personal reflections, and from wandering from the subject. When two or more members rise to speak at the same time, he shall determine which of them is to proceed. When members are, in any respect, out of order, it shall be his duty to call them to order, and in case of refusal to obey, he shall admonish or silence them. He shall prevent members leaving the judicatory without leave obtained from him.

When the deliberations on a particular subject are closed, he shall give a concise and clear statement of the question, take the vote, and announce the result from the chair. If the judicatory be equally divided, he shall have the casting vote; but if he be unwilling to decide, he may put the vote a second time, and if the result be the same, and he still decline to vote, the question shall be lost. He shall appoint all committees, subject to the approval of the judicatory. He shall decide on all points of order, subject, however, to the judgment of the judicatory, and shall have the power of briefly commenting on them, without leaving the chair; but if he would speak on any subject under deliberation, he must invite some other member to preside till he has concluded his remarks. On any extraordinary emergency, he shall be empowered to convene the judicatory, by his circular letter, before the ordinary time of meeting.

6. The clerk shall keep a roll of the standing members of the judicatory; shall call it at the opening of each meeting; enter the names of those present on a distinct roll, to be called at the opening of each sitting, and record the transactions of the court under the direction of the moderator. He shall preserve the records and all papers not otherwise disposed of, and deliver them to his suc-

cessor in office, and furnish the moderator with a list of all unfinished business, and of all papers presented to the judicatory. He shall furnish extracts from the records, and copies of papers, when properly required; and such papers, under the hand of the clerk, shall be considered authentic vouchers of the fact or facts which they declare, in any ecclesiastical judicatory, and to every part of this church. He shall not, without an order from the court, let the original documents go out of his hands.

CHAPTER XI.

OF ORGANIZATION.

UNDER the general head of organization may be included the erection of congregations, admission of members, licensure of probationers, election of church officers, ordination, translation of ministers, and the dissolution of the pastoral relation.

ARTICLE I.

OF THE ERECTION OF CONGREGATIONS.

SECTION 1. As the church increases and extends, it becomes necessary to erect new congregations.

2. This consists in the formation of a number of individuals, agreeing in their religious views, into a regular society, for the support

and enjoyment of all divine ordinances, with some of themselves chosen and ordained to bear office and manage their concerns in a regular and orderly way.

3. When a congregation becomes too numerous conveniently to meet in one place for public worship, or when for any other reason it would promote the cause of religion, and the general interests of the church, to erect a new congregation, the persons so judging shall make application to the presbytery within whose bounds the congregation would be situated, setting forth the necessity and propriety of such erection.

4. If, after hearing the reasons of such application, the presbytery determine to grant it, they shall appoint a minister to carry the object into effect; who, having given due notice to the persons who are to compose the new congregation, of the time and place of meeting for said purpose, and having at the same time and place observed the usual exercises of public worship, shall proceed to hold an election for the proper officers.

5. When the persons who are to compose the congregation are already members of the church in full communion, the election of officers, whether ruling elders or deacons, shall be conducted as in congregations already organized, as prescribed in Article IV., Sec. 4—7 of this chapter.

6. But when the applicants are not in communion, or not a sufficient number of them to afford an opportunity of making a suitable selection, as may be the case, especially in missionary districts, the minister appointed shall first converse individually with all who propose to unite in forming the congregation; and being satisfied with their religious attainments and character, he shall, on the day appointed for the organization, publicly receive their accession, by proposing to them the questions hereinafter prescribed in Article II., Sec. 5. The election shall then be conducted in the usual way, none being entitled to vote, or eligible to office, who have not been received into the communion of the church.

7. When the election is over, the minister shall announce to the congregation the names of the persons duly elected; and on their agreeing to accept the office, and having been examined by him as to their qualifications for, and their views in undertaking the office to which they are about to be set apart, a day shall be appointed for their ordination, the edict served, and the ordination conducted as in other congregations.

8. The minister presiding shall report to the presbytery his procedure in the case, with the names of the officers that have been chosen and ordained. And these, with the name of

the congregation, shall be entered on the presbytery's list.

ARTICLE II.

OF THE ADMISSION OF CHURCH MEMBERS.

As the peace, unity, purity, and prosperity of the church depend, in a great measure, on the character of her members, the greatest care should be exercised by her officers in the admission of persons to her communion. To prevent disorder, and for the guidance of sessions in this matter, let the following directions be observed.

Section 1. In organized congregations, none are to be admitted to communion but by the session constituted.

2. Persons desirous of admission to the fellowship of the church, should embrace some suitable opportunity of intimating their desire to the pastor, or officiating minister, or to an elder, who shall converse with them in relation to the profession and practice required by the word of God, and the subordinate standards of this church, and shall examine them personally on their religious knowledge and experience; and it shall be the duty of the minister to give to all some convenient opportunity for this, previous to every dispensation of the sacrament of the Lord's supper.

3. The minister or elder shall then report,

without delay, the names of applicants, and the result of his examination to the session, that they may have time to inquire into the character and conversation of the applicants. If any of the applicants cannot be attested by some member of session, as to their moral character, it will be the duty of the session to require of them some satisfactory voucher of good moral character; and such further examination shall then be had, as the session may judge necessary, to determine their right to membership as communicants.

4. The same regulation shall be observed with respect to the applications from persons from other denominations, and from members who have been more than a year absent, at a distance from the congregation, and do not produce satisfactory testimonials; or who have been debarred, by a judicial sentence, from the communion of the church, and are desirous of readmission.

5. The session being satisfied respecting the knowledge, principles, motives and character of applicants, shall then take their engagement, by their answering affirmatively the following formula of questions in presence of the session alone, or, which is earnestly recommended, in presence of the congregation, viz.:

1. Do you believe the Scriptures of the Old and New Testaments to be the word of

God, the infallible and only rule of faith and practice?

2. Do you profess your adherence to the doctrines set forth and received by this church, in the Confession of Faith, Catechisms Larger and Shorter, and Declarations of the Testimony, and to the form of presbyterial church government, so far as you have been enabled to understand them, as agreeable to, and founded on the word of God?

3. Do you profess your resolution through grace to continue in the faith; to be subject to the order and discipline of God's house; to be diligent in your attendance upon divine ordinances, both teaching and sealing, according to your profession; on secret prayer, on family worship, as you may have opportunity, or, (if the applicant be the head of a family,) in observing family worship, and in the performance of all other duties incumbent on you, whatever station you may occupy in life; that you will study to promote the peace, purity, and prosperity of this congregation, while you remain a member thereof; and that you will make conscience of promoting the knowledge of Christ and his truth, as by other means, so especially by a holy and godly conversation?

6. After proposing the above questions, let the moderator address a word of exhortation to the newly admitted members, setting before them the importance of the relation

into which they have entered, and the necessity of their seeking the sustaining grace of God.

ARTICLE III.

OF LICENSURE.

SECTION 1. The Holy Scriptures require that trial be previously made of those who are to be ordained to the gospel ministry, that this sacred office be not committed to weak and unworthy men; 1 Tim. iii. 6, not a novice, 2 Tim. ii. 2, and that the churches may have opportunity to judge of the qualifications of those by whom they are to be instructed and governed. To this end, presbyteries shall license probationers to preach the gospel, that after a competent trial of their gifts, and having received a good report from the churches, they may be ordained to the sacred office. 1 Tim. iii. 7, 3 John 12.

2. In ordinary cases, no student of theology can be admitted to trials for license, until he has completed a course of theological study of three full years, after the time of his admission by the presbytery, nor without producing testimonials of unexceptionable conduct, diligence, and proficiency in his studies.

3. When a student of theology has completed the prescribed course of studies, with due proficiency, he shall be taken on trials by that presbytery under whose care he is placed.

4. That the holy ministry be not intrusted to weak and ignorant men, 1 Tim. iii. 6, 7, 2 Tim. ii. 2, 3 John 12, the presbytery shall examine each candidate as to his knowledge of the Latin language, and of the original languages in which the scriptures were written. They shall examine him on the ordinary branches of literature and science, on theology, natural and revealed; on the nature of the sacraments, ecclesiastical history, church government, and the distinguishing principles of our religious profession. And to make trials of his talents to explain, vindicate and practically enforce the doctrines of the gospel, the presbytery shall require him to deliver before them the following exercises, namely:

1. An Exegesis.
2. A Homily.
3. A Critical Exercise.
4. A Lecture.
5. A Popular Sermon.

5. Wherever convenient, it is expedient that these or similar pieces of trial be delivered before the presbytery at different times, that they may be able to judge of the progress of the candidate. But the lecture and popular sermon are to be delivered in public, and immediately before licensure.

6. The presbytery shall also examine the candidate respecting his experimental acquaintance with religion, and his motives in

desiring to enter into the work of the gospel ministry. Rom. ii. 21, 1 Tim. iii. 6, 2 Tim. ii. 2.

7. The presbytery being satisfied with all the parts of the candidate's trials, and having sustained them for license, and having decided to license him, the moderator shall propose to him the formula of questions, (see Art. V.) except such as necessarily imply investiture with office. After answering the questions proposed in a satisfactory manner, he is to be licensed in the name of the Lord Jesus Christ to preach the everlasting gospel as a probationer for the holy ministry. It is proper that the moderator accompany the act of licensure with a suitable word of exhortation.

8. A certificate, which shall be an extract of the official record of licensure, signed by the moderator and clerk of the presbytery, shall be given to probationers.*

9. All probationers shall be under the direction, and fulfil the appointments given by the presbytery by which they were licensed, or into whose bounds they may be regularly sent.

10. When a licentiate shall have been preaching for a considerable time, and his services do not appear to be edifying to the churches, the presbytery may, in their discretion, recall his license.

* See Appendix No. VI.

ARTICLE IV.

OF THE ELECTION OF CHURCH OFFICERS.

Though the authority by which the officers of the church hold their respective offices is conferred through ordination, their right to exercise their office statedly in any congregation, depends on their election by the people.

PART I.—ELECTION OF ELDERS AND DEACONS.

SECTION 1. In settled congregations it is the province of the existing session to judge when an election of additional elders may be necessary, and of the session and deacons to judge when an election of deacons may be necessary, and to proceed to such election without an application to the presbytery.

2. When an election of ruling elders or deacons in any congregation has been appointed, notice shall be given at least ten days previous, that the people may consult among themselves, and fix upon some suitable persons.

3. On the day appointed for the election, which shall be some week day, days of fasting and thanksgiving excepted, after the close of public worship, the moderator shall state the object of the meeting, and after prayer for divine direction, the session having previously agreed upon suitable persons, shall nominate them to the congregation,

yet this shall not preclude the nomination of others by any member of the congregation.

4. None shall be eligible to office, nor are any entitled to vote in such election, but such as are members in full communion in the congregation at the time of the election.

5. Nominations having been made, the vote shall be taken on each candidate separately: it may be taken either with the uplifted hand, or in such manner as the session may approve, care being taken that it be a fair and unbiassed expression of the will of the people; and no person shall be considered as elected unless he have a majority of the whole number of votes given.

6. The result of the election shall be publicly announced by the Moderator, and if it be in a vacant congregation, he shall make report of it to the presbytery as in the case of organization. (See Art. I.)

PART II.—ELECTION OF MINISTERS.

Section 1. When a congregation after hearing a minister or probationer, desire to obtain him for their pastor, the elders shall convene them, that they may petition the presbytery, under whose inspection they are, for the appointment of a member of presbytery to preside in the moderation of a call. They shall also at the same time appoint one or more of their own number to present their petition, and give such information in relation to the situation and prospects of the congregation, and the support which they intend to give their minister, as the presbytery may require.

2. If the moderation be granted, the presbytery shall appoint one of their own number to preach on a week day, as soon as convenient, in the usual place of worship of the said congregation, and to moderate in a call. Due notice of the purpose, time, and place of the meeting shall be given to the congregation. But if, from any unexpected circumstance, a large proportion of the people have been prevented attending on the appointed day, the minister may defer the election another week, without a new order from presbytery.

3. On the day appointed, after the close of public worship, the minister shall state the object of the meeting, read a blank call in the hearing of the congregation, and, after prayer for divine direction, shall call for the nomination of a candidate; then, having twice distinctly announced the name of the nominee, shall call upon all who favour the nomination to hold up their right hands, and afterwards such as are against it. If there is more than one candidate, the presiding minister shall, in the manner just specified, take the vote on each nomination.

4. None are entitled to vote in the elec-

tion of a pastor but such as are in full communion at the time of the election; and no candidate shall be considered as elected who has not a majority of all the votes.

5. After the election, the result shall be announced, the blank in the call filled, and the electors requested to come forward and affix their signatures to the call. It shall be signed, first by the elders and deacons, and then by all the members. The ordinary hearers, though not entitled to vote, may, if they choose, affix their signatures to the call as adherents. The call thus subscribed, witnessed by two or more respectable persons not members of the congregation, if they can be obtained, and attested by the presiding minister, shall be transmitted to the presbytery by a commissioner or commissioners duly appointed.*

6. In case there be a minority opposed to the candidate elect, the Moderator shall endeavour to persuade them to acquiesce in the choice of their brethren. But if this minority be large and steadily refuse to acquiesce, he shall report the facts to the presbytery, that they may judge what is best for the interests and peace of the congregation.

7. The call being now in the hands of the presbytery it must by them be sustained, be-

* For the form of a call, and of its attestation, see Appendix, No. IV. V.

fore presentation to the candidate. And, when it is known or believed that any other presbytery is concerned in the matter, information shall be communicated to said presbytery previous to the presentation.

8. When there are competing calls they shall be transmitted for presentation to the presbytery to which the candidate belongs, or to the Synod, if it is to meet within a reasonable time.

9. No minister or probationer shall receive a call, except through the hands of a presbytery or synod. When a call is presented and accepted the way is open for proceeding to ordination and installation.

ARTICLE V.

OF THE ORDINATION OF CHURCH OFFICERS.

PART I. ORDINATION OF ELDERS AND DEACONS.

SECTION 1. Previous to the ordination of ruling elders and deacons, the session shall meet to examine the officers elect, as to their acceptance of the office, their views in undertaking it, and their qualifications for it.

2. The officers elect having been approved, and having declared their willingness to accept the office, a day shall be appointed for their ordination, and public notice thereof given to the congregation, not less than ten days previous.

3. The public notice of such an appointment shall be accompanied with the serving of an edict, which is a public intimation that if any person has anything to object against the faith or conversation of any of the officers elect, such objection shall be given in by a specified time, otherwise the ordination shall be proceeded with.*

4. No valid objection being offered, after sermon the presiding minister shall briefly narrate the proceedings already had, and, the candidates for ordination presenting themselves before the congregation, he shall propose to them the formula of questions annexed to this article, and these questions being answered in the affirmative, he shall propose to the members of the church, the following questions, viz.:

Do you, the members of this church adhere to your choice of and receive this brother as a ruling elder, or deacon, and do you promise to yield him all that honor, encouragement and obedience, in the Lord, to which his office entitles him?

The members of the church having answered this question in the affirmative, by holding up their right hands, the Moderator shall proceed to set apart the candidates by prayer. After prayer he shall exhort both officers and people to their respective duties.

* For form of edict, see Appendix, No. VII.

5. At the close of the service, it is proper that the members of the existing session, in presence of the congregation, take the newly ordained elder or elders by the hand, saying, "We give unto you the right hand of fellowship, take part of this office with us." And before the session adjourns a record of the ordination shall be inserted in their minutes.

6. An elder or deacon removing from his own into another congregation, and presenting suitable testimonials of his personal and official conduct, shall, on his being duly elected by the congregation, be installed as an elder or deacon without a new ordination.

7. A list of ruling elders in every congregation with the time of their ordination, is to be given by the minister to the presbytery.

PART II. ORDINATION OF MINISTERS.

Section 1. Where a call has been accepted by a probationer, the presbytery shall appoint him trials for ordination. These shall consist of an examination on personal religion, theology, natural and revealed, the original languages of the Holy Scriptures, ecclesiastical history and church government, pastoral duties and the principles of our public profession, together with at least two public discourses, a lecture and a popular sermon.

2. These trials having been passed to the

satisfaction of presbytery, they shall appoint a day for the ordination of the candidate; and shall also cause the congregation to be assembled a convenient time previous thereto, at least ten days; and at that time a written intimation termed an edict shall be publicly read to the congregation, purporting that, "the presbytery having received a call for Mr. A. B. preacher of the gospel, to be their pastor, and finding nothing to hinder his settlement among them, will ordain and install him accordingly, if no just objection be seasonably offered.*

3. The presbytery being met at the time specified in the edict, the person by them appointed to serve it, or, in his absence, the clerk of the congregation, or one of the session, shall return it endorsed with his certification, that it has been duly served. The presbytery shall then direct him to make proclamation in the church that they are now assembled and ready to hear any objection to the life and doctrine of the candidate. If no objection be made the presbytery shall proceed with the ordination; but if any be made, the presbytery shall carefully consider them, and shall either sustain or over-rule them, as their nature and proof shall render necessary.

* See Appendix, No. VII.

4. On the day of ordination a solemn fast shall be observed in the congregation, that they may more earnestly join in public prayer for the Lord's blessing on his ordinances, and on the labors of his servant to whom the administration of these among them is about to be committed.

5. No valid objection to the ordination being offered, a member of presbytery, previously appointed, shall preach a sermon adapted to the occasion. The same, or another member appointed to preside, shall afterwards briefly narrate the proceedings of the presbytery preparatory to this transaction, and shall then request the candidate to present himself. The questions in the annexed formula shall then be proposed to him.

6. Satisfactory answers being given to these questions, the presiding minister shall propose to the people the following questions:

1. Do you, the people of this congregation, still profess your readiness to receive   whom you have called to be your pastor?

2. Do you promise to receive the word of truth from his mouth, with meekness and love; and to submit to him in the due exercise of discipline? Jas. i. 21, Heb. xiii. 17.

3. Do you promise to encourage him in his labors for your instruction and edification? 1 Thes. v. 12, 13. And do you engage to give him, while he is your pastor, that competent worldly maintenance which you have promised, and whatever else you may see to be needful for the honor of religion, and his comfort among you? 1 Cor. ix. 7-15.

4. The people having answered these questions in the affirmative, by holding up their right hands, the candidate shall kneel. Then the presiding minister shall, by prayer, Acts xiii. 2, 3, and with the laying on of the hands of the presbytery, 1 Tim. iv. 14, solemnly ordain him to the office of the holy ministry. Prayer being ended, the presiding minister first, and the other members in order, shall take him by the right hand, saying, "We give you the right hand of fellowship, to take part of this ministry with us." Gal. ii. 9, Acts i. 25. An appropriate charge shall then be delivered to both pastor and people; 2 Tim. iv. 1, 2., Mark iv. 24. After praying and singing, the congregation shall be dismissed in the usual manner, and then invited to come forward, and in token of their regard, take their minister by the hand. The whole transaction shall be recorded in the presbytery's book.*

* See Appendix No. VIII.

8. Installation, which is the establishment of the relation between a pastor and his flock, shall always accompany ordination when a call has been accepted.

9. As in particular emergencies, it may be desirable and necessary that a licentiate be ordained to the gospel ministry without a pastoral charge, in such case the questions of the formula having reference to a pastoral charge must be modified according to the circumstances.

FORMULA OF QUESTIONS FOR MINISTERS, RULING ELDERS AND DEACONS AT THEIR ORDINATION.

1. Do you believe the holy Scriptures of the Old and New Testaments to be the word of the living God, the infallible and only rule of faith and practice? 2 Tim. iii. 16, Eph. ii. 20.

2. Do you believe and acknowledge the doctrines professed by this church, and contained in the Confession of Faith, Catechisms Larger and Shorter, and the Declarations of the Testimony, to be founded on the word of God, and are you resolved through divine grace, to maintain and adhere to the same, in opposition to all errors, and against all contrary opinions? 2 Tim. i. 13.

3. Do you approve the Form of Presbyterial Church Government, and the Directories for worship, received by this church, as

agreeable to, and founded on the word of God; and are you resolved by the grace of God, to maintain and defend the same against all contrary opinions?

4. Do you promise to submit, in the spirit of meekness, to the admonitions of the brethren of this presbytery, (or of this session) in subordination to the Synod and General Assembly, 1 Peter v. 15; and do you promise to maintain the unity of the Spirit in the bond of peace; that you will not follow divisive courses, either by complying with the defections of the times, or giving yourself (or yourselves) up to a detestable neutrality in the cause of God? Acts xx. 17-31.

5. Are not zeal for the glory of God, love to the Lord Jesus, and a desire of being useful in edifying the church of Christ, the chief motives which induce you to accept the office of a pastor (or ruling elder or deacon) in this congregation? 1 Cor. ii. 2, 2 Cor. iv. 5.

6. Have you used any undue methods to procure your call to the office of pastor, (ruling elder or deacon) in this congregation?

7. Do you promise through grace, to endeavor, as much as lieth in your power, to perform all the official duties incumbent on you with zeal and fidelity; and that you will be circumspect in your whole conversation,

following after righteousness, faith, charity? Epistles to Tim. and Titus.

FOR MINISTERS.

8. Are you now willing to take charge of this congregation, agreeably to your declaration at accepting their call; and do you promise to perform all the duties of a pastor to them, preaching the gospel, not with enticing words of man's wisdom, but in the purity and simplicity thereof; not shunning to declare the whole counsel of God; to catechise and exhort from house to house; to visit the sick; and to perform whatever other duties are incumbent upon you, as a faithful minister of Christ, for the convincing and reclaiming of sinners, and for building up saints in their most holy faith?

FOR RULING ELDERS.

9. Do you now accept the call to the office of ruling elder in this congregation, agreeably to your former declaration; and do you promise, through grace, diligently to discharge all the duties of that office; to be faithful and impartial in the exercise of discipline, and to be punctual in attending the meetings of session, and superior judicatories, as you may be required? 1 Pet. v. 2.

FOR DEACONS.

10. Do you now accept of the call to the office of deacon in this congregation, agreeably to your former declaration; and do

you promise to attend to the wants of the poor, with Christian meekness and tenderness, and to manage all such temporalities of the church as may be committed to your care with diligence and fidelity, according to the concurrent advice and directions of the session?

FOR MINISTERS, ELDERS, AND DEACONS.

11. Do you make these promises as in the presence of the living God, who searcheth the hearts, and trieth the reins of the children of men, and as you would desire to give in your account with joy, at the great day of the Redeemer's appearance, when he shall come, and all his saints with him, to judge the quick and the dead?

ARTICLE VI.

OF THE TRANSLATION OF MINISTERS.

Section 1. As a minister of the gospel is by his office related to the whole church, he may, for sufficient reasons, be removed from one pastoral charge to another.

2. No minister shall be translated from one charge to another, nor shall he receive a call for that purpose, but by the authority of the presbytery or synod of which he is a member.

3. The important interests that are involved in the translation of a minister, and

the danger of creating jealousies and dissensions, by which the peace and comfort of the church may be disturbed, render it obligatory on presbyteries to proceed with great caution, deliberation, and tenderness towards all parties interested.

4. A call for a settled minister shall be prepared and prosecuted in the same manner as one for a probationer or minister without charge.

5. Before presenting a call to a minister who is pastor of another congregation, the presbytery shall require the congregation calling, by their commissioners, to represent to the presbytery the grounds on which they ask for his translation. They shall also summon the congregation, whose minister is called, to appear at their next meeting, to show cause, by their commissioners or in writing, why the call should not be presented and the translation take place. This citation shall be read from the pulpit of that church, by a member of presbytery, or some other suitable person appointed by presbytery, immediately after public worship; so that at least two Sabbaths shall intervene between the citation and the meeting of presbytery at which the matter is to be heard. If the congregation send no representation by commissioners or otherwise, against the removal of their pastor, and if the presbytery are satisfied with the reasons as-

signed for the proposed translation, they shall forthwith present the call, and if it be accepted, they shall dissolve the pastoral relation already existing, and translate the candidate to the other congregation. The day of his installation shall be fixed, and the edict appointed to be served. But if the congregation whose pastor is called oppose the removal, the presbytery shall hear the parties, and after careful and serious deliberation, either continue him in his present charge, or translate him, as they deem most for the edification of the church; or they may refer the whole matter to the synod, for advice and direction.

6. When the minister called belongs to a different presbytery, the presbytery, which has sustained the call, shall transmit it, together with a statement of the grounds on which his translation is asked for, to the presbytery of which he is a member, that it may be presented, or they may authorize the congregation to prosecute the call, by their commissioners, before that presbytery, and that presbytery having cited him and his congregation, shall proceed to hear and issue the cause, as before directed. If they agree to his translation, they shall release him from his charge; and having given him proper testimonials, signed by the moderator and clerk, direct him to repair to the presbytery, with-

in whose bounds the congregation calling him lies, that the proper steps may be taken for his settlement. The presbytery to which the congregation belongs, having received a certificate of his release, shall proceed to install him in his new charge as soon as practicable. No pastor shall be translated without his own consent.

7. Installation, which consists in constituting a pastoral relation between a minister and the people of a particular church, may, in case of a minister previously ordained, be performed by the presbytery, or a committee appointed for that purpose, and the following order shall be observed therein:—

8. A day shall be appointed for the instalment, and due notice thereof shall be given to the congregation. The presbytery or a committee having met on the day appointed, they shall proceed as in the case of ordination and installation. The member who presides shall then address himself to the minister to be installed, proposing to him the 6th, 7th and 8th questions of the formula for the ordination of ministers, together with the following:

"And all this you promise in agreeableness to your ordination engagements, and in humble reliance upon divine grace?"

Having received satisfactory answers to all these, he shall propose to the people the questions prescribed in Article V., Part II., Section 6, which having been answered in the affirmative, by holding up the right hand, he shall solemnly declare said minister to be regularly constituted pastor of that congregation. A charge shall then be given to both parties, and after prayer and singing a psalm, the congregation shall be dismissed with the usual benediction.

9. It is highly proper that after the services, the officers and other members of the congregation should come forward to their pastor, and give him the right hand, in token of their cordial reception and affectionate regard.

10. The presbytery shall always enter upon their minutes their reasons for translating a minister; and when that act is likely to give much dissatisfaction to his people, a copy of these reasons shall be extracted and sent to them by their commissioners.

ARTICLE VII.

DISSOLUTION OF THE PASTORAL RELATION.

Section 1. As the authority of the presbytery is interposed in the formation of the pastoral relation, so it shall be necessary to its dissolution.

2. When circumstances arise which seem to render a dissolution of the pastoral relation necessary, application to this end may

be made either by the pastor or people, or by both united, and shall in all cases be accompanied with a statement of the reasons for which it is urged.

3. If the application be made by the pastor, the congregation shall be cited to appear, as in the case of translation, and if the application be from the congregation, the pastor shall be cited to appear, and show cause why the application should not be granted. As this is a matter important in its nature and consequences, the presbytery shall give it the same careful and serious deliberation prescribed in the matter of translation from one charge to another.

4. If, upon due consideration of the case, the presbytery shall judge it for edification to grant the petition, the congregation shall be declared vacant, and the minister who has thus been released shall remain subject to the orders of the presbytery.

PART II.

OF DISCIPLINE.

CHAPTER I.

GENERAL PRINCIPLES.

SECTION 1. Discipline is the exercise of that authority with which the Lord Jesus Christ has clothed the officers of his house, in the application of the laws which he has given in his word. Acts xv. 25—29; Rev. ii. 2, 3.

2. The exercise of discipline is most necessary, because in the imperfect and mingled state of the visible church, disorders will arise, not only among carnal professors, but also, from remaining corruption, among the truly gracious. Matt. xviii. 7, 15—17. Its general object is the removal of offences, and preventing their unhappy effects. The special designs are, vindicating the honor and authority of Jesus Christ, Ezek. xxii. 26; xliv. 6–8; maintaining the purity of his ordinances and of his truth, Rev. ii. 2, 3, averting judgments which are threatened on account of offences connived at, Rev. ii. 5, 16, preserving the cause of God for posterity, Rev. ii. 5; Ps.

lxxviii. 5—8; reclaiming offenders, 1 Cor. v. 5, warning others that they may fear, 1 Tim. v. 20, and promoting the peace and edification of the body of Chist.

3. An offence, the ground of discipline, is anything in the avowed belief, or in the practice of a church member which is contrary to the word of God, and the standards of the United Presbyterian Church; or which in its nature and circumstances is calculated to lead others into sin. Rom. xiv. 13, 20, 21; Rev. ii. 14. Nothing, therefore, ought to be considered by any judicatory as an offence, or admitted as a ground of censure, which cannot be shown to be such from the word of God, and the regulations and practice of the church, or which does not involve those evils for the prevention of which discipline is intended.

4. The proper exercise of discipline requires, in the office-bearers of the church, not only fidelity and firmness, but also tenderness and moderation, wisdom and discrimination. Scandals of the same kind cannot always be treated in the same manner, in consequence of the different circumstances that may attend them, rendering them more or less offensive; and which may therefore require a different mode of procedure in similar cases, at different times, for the attainment of the same end. 1 Tim. i. 20; Gal. v. 12; Jude 22, 23.

5. All baptized persons, being members of the church, are under her care and subject to her authority and discipline: and having attained the years of discretion are bound to perform all the duties of church members.

CHAPTER II.

OF OFFENCES.

Section 1. Offences are either personal or general, and these may be either private or public: and the procedure will vary in some respects, in reference to these several classes.

2. A personal offence is a violation of the Divine law, considered in the character of a wrong or injury done to a particular individual or individuals. A general offence is any heresy or immorality having no personal relation, or apart from it. While, therefore, a general offence may not be personal, every personal offence is general.

3. Private offences are such as are known only to an individual, or at most, to a few persons. Public offences are such as are generally known, or are known to many persons.

CHAPTER III.

OF THE PARTIES IN CASES OF PROCESS.

Section 1. In cases of personal offences the injured party, whether the offence be public or private, must first use the means prescribed by our Lord, Matt. xviii. 15—17, of bringing the offender to a sense of his error, and effecting a reconciliation, before he can be admitted as a prosecutor. He must go to him privately and alone, and endeavor to bring him to an acknowledgment of his sin, and to sorrow for it. If in this he succeed, the matter shall terminate. But if he at first fail, he must continue his dealing, taking with him others, who may unite with him in, and be evidences of his Christian expostulations; failing here he is to tell it to the church. Failure to comply with our Lord's direction, by any one lodging information against another, is itself an offence subjecting the informer to censure. As, however, the interests of religion may require a judicial investigation of a personal offence, as general, the settlement of the matter between the parties shall not preclude a church court from investigating it.

2. In all cases of private offences, though they be general, he or they to whom they are known, are bound to use the above named private means for the removal of the scandal, and no one can be admitted as an accuser who has not complied with this rule. Where a private offence is known only to an individual, and is therefore not susceptible of legal proof, it is, after serious and close dealing, to be left between God and the offender's conscience.

3. General offences may be brought before a judicatory either by an individual or individuals appearing as accusers, and undertaking to substantiate the charge, or by information, where the informer declines to appear as a prosecutor, or by a common fame.

4. In prosecutions by common fame, the previous steps required by our Lord in relation to personal offences, are not necessary. Yet, even here, an offence may be so circumstanced as to render it proper for the court to appoint a committee of inquiry, in order to ascertain whether the case be such as requires judicial investigation, and can be prosecuted to conviction, and also to converse with the offender, and endeavor to bring him to a sense of his sin, without actual process.

5. Taking up charges on the ground of common fame, requires caution and prudence on the part of the judicatory, inasmuch as it is not every report that amounts to this. It must first be determined that a common fame really exists, and no rumor is to be regarded as such, unless it specify some particular sin or sins, is general or widely spread, is not transient but permanent, generally believed, and accompanied with a strong presumption of truth.

6. As, however, a rumor may exist, not amounting to common fame, affecting the character of an individual, the person affected

thereby may request a judicial investigation for his own vindication, and it may be proper for the judicatory to grant the request.

7. In cases taken up on information, the name of the informer is not to be given up without his consent; but if the innocence of the party accused be clearly made out, the judicatory shall inquire whether the information was lodged through malice, or imprudence, or otherwise, and deal with him accordingly.

8. In all cases of process on the ground of common fame, or by information, where the informer refuses to appear, the judicatory may appoint an individual member of the court to act as prosecutor in the management of the case. A session may appoint any person who is a church member and under their jurisdiction.

9. All charges must be drawn up in the form of libel or complaint. A libel is a written charge preferred against an individual or individuals, in argumentative form. It first specifies the offence as censurable, and cites authorities from Scripture and the standards of the church to prove this, then charges the offence in point of fact on the accused by name, including, as far as practicable, a specification of time and place, and concludes with the inference that he ought to be cen-

sured.* A complaint differs from this in omitting the first part, in other respects it is the same; and as the relevancy of the charge must be determined by the court, the latter form is sufficient in all ordinary cases. In either form the offence must be distinctly specified, with times and places as far as practicable, and the names of witnesses.

10. The original and only parties to a trial are the accuser and the accused; and in cases where the court appoints the accuser, he shall exercise all the rights of an original party. These parties shall be known in the appellate courts as the appellant and appellee.

11. In reciving charges, no person can be admitted as an accuser who is known to indulge an evil spirit towards the accused, is not of good fame, is under process or censure, is deeply interested in the conviction of the accused; and great caution should be exercised where the accuser is rash, litigious, or imprudent. Persons who appear as accusers, or who undertake to substantiate a charge, shall be held subject to censure if they fail in proof, unless it appear that there were strong presumptions of the guilt of the accused.

* See Appendix, No. 11.

CHAPTER IV.

OF ACTUAL PROCESS.

SECTION 1. When all other means of removing an offence have failed, the judicatory, which has immediate cognizance of it, shall judicially take it into consideration. But at the first meeting of the judicatory, when a libel or complaint has been tabled, no further proceedings shall be had, unless by consent of parties, than to furnish the accused with a copy of the libel or complaint, and a list of the witnesses annexed, and to cite all concerned to appear at the next meeting of the judicatory. Notice shall be given to the parties and witnesses at least ten days previous to the meeting of the judicatory, and if the parties be present when the charge is received, and the time and place of trial appointed, that shall be held as sufficient citation and notification.

2. If the accused party be absent when the charge is received and trial appointed, a citation with notification of time and place of trial, and a list of witnesses, shall be put into his hands, or left at the usual place of his residence, by some suitable person appointed for the purpose.* Citations shall also be issued to such witnesses as the accused shall name, who are members of the

* See Appendix, No. 12.

church, to appear on his behalf.* And all citations shall be signed in the name of the judicatory, by the moderator and clerk. Other persons can only be requested to attend.

3. In drawing up charges, times, places, and circumstances should, if possible, be particularly stated, that the accused may have an opportunity of proving an *alibi*, or explaining admitted facts in extenuation or justification of them; and every libel or complaint, except those founded on common fame, must be thus specific.

4. If an accused person neglects or refuses to obey the citation, he is to be cited a second time, and, if this be not answered, a third time, with notification that if he do not appear, or send a sufficient excuse, the judicatory will proceed to trial as if he were present, and also censure him for his contumacy.

5. While the time intervening between the first citation of an accused person and the meeting of the judicatory at which he is to appear, must be at least ten days, the time allowed on a subsequent citation, is in the discretion of the court; provided always, however, that it be sufficient for a convenient compliance. And in every case of unusual

* See Appendix, No. 13.

distance from, or difficulty of communication with the place of meeting, a reasonable time shall always be allowed.

6. The judicatory, before proceeding to trial, shall ascertain that their citations have been duly served, and especially before they judge a person guilty of contumacy or inflict any censure for it.

7. Before proceeding to trial, the first point to be determined is, the admissibility of the charges. In most cases this will have been done before the citation of the accused, yet, as he has a right to be heard on that point, and may not be present to plead to it, and as it may be affected, not only by the position and character of the accuser, but also by the inadmissibility of the testimony and the general and indefinite character of the charges, it ought not, in some cases, to be regarded as definitely settled till the accused be heard. If the charges be judged inadmissible, all further proceedings cease.

8. The first thing to be considered on the trial is the relevancy of the libel, that is, whether the charges, if proved, be censurable. On this, the accused, if present, has a right to be fully heard, but not in making a plea against the principles of his public profession. If, on careful consideration, the charges be found not relevant, all further proceedings must terminate; but if they are

sustained as relevant, the accused is to be interrogated as to the matters of fact. If he admit them, the way is open for a decision, but if he deny them, the judicatory shall proceed with the trial.

9. The trial shall be fair and impartial. The witnesses shall be examined in presence of the accused, or at least after he has received due citation to attend; and he shall be permitted to cross-examine them, and to ask any question tending to his own exculpation. After all the evidence has been taken in confirmation of the charge, the accused shall introduce whatever rebutting or extenuating evidence he has to offer.

10. The testimony being closed, the accused shall be heard first, and then the accuser, and the court shall decide whether the accused shall have an opportunity of being further heard. The parties being removed, the judicatory shall proceed to examine and weigh the testimony, and give judgment accordingly.

11. The judgment shall be regularly entered on the records of the judicatory, and the parties shall be allowed copies of the whole proceedings, at their own expense, if they demand them; and in case of the removal of a cause to a higher court, the lower judicatory shall send a complete authenticated copy of the whole record to the higher judicatory.

12. The sentence, if it is thought necessary to publish it, shall be published only in the church or churches which have been offended; but when the ends of public edification can be as well answered, private censure is to be preferred.

13. As cases may arise in which a considerable time may intervene before it is practicable to commence process against an accused church member, the session may, in such cases, if they think it necessary to edification, prevent the accused from approaching the Lord's table until the charges against him can be examined. And if an individual be evading process, the judicatory shall enter that fact on its records, together with the nature of the offence charged, and shall suspend him from all church privileges until he appear before the court and answer to the charges against him.

14. If the testimony taken during a trial, proves a sin, properly denominated by another name than that designated in the libel, while the specific charge of the libel must be found not proved, the accused may be found guilty of that which appears in proof, and sentence passed accordingly, provided, nevertheless, that further time shall be given to him for defence, if he demand it, or justice require it.

15. No professional counsel shall be per-

mitted to appear and plead in cases of process in any of our ecclesiastical courts; but an accused person may, if he desire it, be represented by any member of the church, subject to the jurisdiction of the court before which he appears. The person so employed, if a member of the court, shall not be allowed, after pleading the cause of the accused, to sit in judgment on the case.

16. Questions of order, which arise in the course of process, shall be decided by the Moderator. If an appeal is made from the decision of the chair, the question on appeal shall be taken without debate. Decisions on points of order shall always be recorded, if either party shall request it.

17. The records of the proceedings, in cases of judicial process, shall exhibit not only the charges, specifications, and sentence of the court, but all the testimony and all the circumstances which had an influence on its judgment; and nothing which is not contained in the record shall be taken into consideration in reviewing the proceedings in a higher court.

CHAPTER V.

OF PROCESS AGAINST MINISTERS.

Section 1. As the honor and success of the gospel is intimately connected with the unblemished reputation of its ministers, both as to doctrine and conduct, each presbytery should take special care that charges are not received against them on slight or frivolous grounds; nor, when received, are they to be negligently examined, or slightly censured if found true.

2. Process against a gospel minister shall always be entered before the presbytery of which he is a member, and the rules of procedure laid down in Chapter IV., under the head of Actual Process, are to be strictly observed in every process against a minister. Process against a licentiate shall be entered, if practicable, before the presbytery in whose bounds he is laboring, and if not, before the presbytery under whose care he is.

3. If the offence with which a minister stands charged occurred without the bounds of his own presbytery, that presbytery shall send notice to the presbytery within whose bounds it did occur; and request them either to cite the witnesses to appear at the place of trial, if within convenient distance, or, if the distance be so great as to render attendance inconvenient, to take the examination themselves and transmit an authentic record of their testimony; always giving due notice to the accused person of the time and place of such examination.

4. When a minister is supposed to be guilty of an offence, at such a distance from the

place of his residence, as that it is not likely to become otherwise known to the presbytery to which he belongs, in such case, it shall be the duty of the presbytery in whose bounds the facts have happened, after satisfying themselves that there is sufficient ground of accusation, to send notice to the presbytery of which he is a member, which is to proceed against him, and request the other presbytery to take the testimony as in preceding section, or they may send a commissioner appointed by themselves for this purpose. In either case due notice must be given to the accused party.

5. Process shall not be commenced against a minister unless at the instance of a responsible party who undertakes to prove the charge; or unless common fame so loudly proclaims the scandal that the presbytery find it necessary to investigate the charge. And where there is a prosecutor, he should be previously informed that if he fail to show probable cause for the charges, he must himself be censured as a slanderer of the gospel ministry, in proportion to the malignity and rashness that may appear in the prosecution.

6. Persons aggrieved by ministers are required to acquaint them with their grievances in private, whether the offences have been public or private, and failing to obtain satisfaction, to apply to some other minister of the

presbytery for his advice in the case, before they can be admitted to present a complaint or libel to the presbytery.

7. Every complaint or libel must be reduced to writing before it is laid before the presbytery. And after receiving it, the presbytery shall act according to the regulations laid down, Chapter IV., Section 1, under the head of actual process.

8. At the next meeting the charge shall be read to the minister accused, and he shall be called upon to say whether he is guilty or not. If he confess, the presbytery shall deal with him according to their discretion; if he plead and take issue, the trial shall proceed, as directed in Chapter IV., Sections 7—10. If found guilty, he shall be censured according to the degree of his offence.

9. If, on the trial, it appear that the matter complained of amounts to no more than acts of infirmity which may be amended, and the people satisfied, so that little remains to hinder his usefulness, they shall take all prudent measures for the removal of the offence.

10. A minister who has been accused of scandal, being twice duly cited, and refusing to attend the presbytery, shall be immediately suspended.

11. A minister, under process for scandal, shall retain, unimpaired, his right to deliberate and vote in other matters, unless the

scandal charged be of such a nature that the presbytery consider it necessary to suspend him from the exercise of his ministry till the charge be investigated.

CHAPTER VI.

OF EXCEPTIONAL CASES.

SECTION 1. There are cases in which the guilt of an individual is manifest, the offence being committed in the presence of the court, or in which trial is rendered unnecessary by the confession of the party; in such cases judgment may be given without process.

2. As there is no accuser in such cases, if the sentence of the judicatory be appealed from, some person, a member of the court, or a member of the church, and subject to the jurisdiction of the same court with the appellant, shall be appointed to defend the sentence in the superior court, and such person shall be the appellee in the case.

CHAPTER VII.

OF EVIDENCE.

SECTION 1. A charge of scandal may be established by the testimony of witnesses, by the records of a church court, or by written or published papers.

2. In receiving the testimony of witnesses, great care and impartiality should be exer-

cised by judicatories. All persons are not competent as witnesses, and all who are competent are not credible.

3. Incompetency is either absolute or relative. A witness who does not believe in the existence of God, or in a future state of rewards and punishments, or is an idiot, is absolutely incompetent. Relative incompetency arises from a want of proper age or intelligence, a defect in any of the senses, or things of a like character. Either party has a right to challenge a witness whom he believes to be incompetent, and the court shall examine and decide on his competency.

4. The credibility of witnesses, or the degree of credit to be given to their testimony, may be affected by their relationship to either of the parties; by interest in the result; by infamy of character; by enmity to the accused; by being under censure for scandal or process for scandal impeaching their veracity; by general rashness, indiscretion, or malignity of character; and by various other circumstances; to which judicatories should carefully attend, and for which they should make due allowance in their decision.

5. A husband or wife shall not be compelled to bear witness for or against each other; nor when either of them is a party directly interested in the result, shall the

other be a witness, except when the offence is committed by the one against the other.

6. When the proof of a charge depends entirely upon the testimony of witnesses, two credible witnesses, at least, shall be necessary to establish the fact or facts charged. Deut. xix. 15. But if several different witnesses bear testimony to different similar acts belonging to the same general charge, or to circumstances necessarily connected with the truth of the fact or facts, the crime shall be considered proved. Ex. xxii. 10—13; Deut. xxii. 23—27; 1 Kings iii. 16—27.

7. A member of the judicatory may be called upon to bear testimony in a case which comes before it. He shall be qualified as other witnesses are; and, after giving his testimony, may resume his seat as a member of the judicatory.

8. Witnesses, afterward to be examined, except members of the judicatory, shall not be present during the examination of another witness, if either party demand their exclusion.

9. Witnesses before giving their testimony, are, if it be required, to be solemnly purged of malice against the accused; and no testimony shall be received but on oath, except by consent of parties.

10. After a witness has been sworn,* he

* See Appendix. No. XIV.

shall be requested first to state what he knows of the matter charged; if he decline this method, or having given his statement, he shall be examined by the party introducing him; then cross-examined by the opposite party; after which any member of the judicatory, or either party may put additional interrogatories. The court shall not permit frivolous questions, or questions not pertinent to the charge at issue, and every question must be put through the moderator.

11. Every question put to a witness shall, if required, be reduced to writing. When answered, it, together with the answer, shall be recorded, if either party require it.

12. The testimony given by witnesses shall be faithfully recorded, read to them for correction and approval, and then being subscribed by them, shall be attested by the moderator.

13. A member of the church summoned as a witness, and refusing to appear, or having appeared, refusing to give testimony, may be censured for contumacy.

14. The records of a church court, or any part of them, whether original or transcribed, attested by the moderator and clerk, or either of them, shall be admitted as legal evidence in every other judicatory. And in like manner, testimony taken by one judicatory at the request of another, shall be re-

ceived by the latter as though it had been taken by themselves.

15. Private writings and printed publications, the genuineness and authorship of which are clearly established, may also be received in evidence.

16. Where it may not be practicable to take a part, or the whole of the testimony of the witnesses in the presence of the court, on account of their distance from the place of meeting, or the impossibility of any of them attending in person, commissioners shall be appointed to take the testimony in question; of which commission, and the time and place of meeting, due notice shall be given to the opposite party, that they may attend. And if the accused party shall, on his part, desire to take testimony under similar circumstances, he shall give notice to the judicatory of the time and place when and where it is proposed to take it, that a commission, as in the former case, may be appointed for the purpose. All testimony thus taken shall be regarded as if taken in the presence of the judicatory.

17. All evidence is either positive or circumstantial. Positive evidence is that by which the fact, charged as a crime, is directly proven. Circumstantial evidence is that which proves such circumstances as necessarily or usually attend, or which have a tendency to establish such facts.

18. The evidence of a fact arising from circumstances necessarily connected with it, is called *violent presumption*. Such presumption only can be admitted as sufficient evidence; and, even then, it must be of such a nature as to produce full conviction on the minds of the judicatory. But while, in some cases, violent presumption may produce as strong conviction as can be got in any other way, the greatest caution and circumspection are always to be used in admitting them, especially in the absence of the positive testimony of at least one credible witness.

19. The evidence of a fact arising from circumstances which usually attend, or which have a tendency to establish it, is called *probable presumption;* this, though it has various degrees of weight, may be destroyed by contrary presumptions equally probable. Such presumption can only serve to corroborate other evidence; of itself it is not sufficient proof of a fact.

20. The positive testimony of a witness often affords nothing more than a probable presumption of a fact, as when there is manifest reason to doubt his veracity, or his right apprehension of the facts which he gives in testimony, or the accuracy of his memory, or when his testimony is contradicted by a witness equally positive and credible. The ju-

dicatory is therefore not bound, by their admission of a witness, to give judgment according to his testimony.

21. When a witness gives his testimony as merely his opinion, his strong impression, or his uncertain remembrance, it is only probable evidence. When, however, a witness gives his opinion, he should be asked to state the reasons on which it is founded.

22. No *second-hand* or *hearsay* testimony is to be received, unless that which goes to prove the statements of persons who would have been credible witnesses, but are deceased; and it shall rest with the judicatory whether they will receive it or not, and what weight to allow it, if received.

23. No private knowledge possessed by members of the judicatory, shall be suffered to influence the decision, as that must be based upon what is actually in evidence.

24. If, in the prosecution of an appeal, new testimony is offered, the appellate court may, if they find the evidence to be important in its bearing on the case, to have been unknown, or wholly beyond the reach of the party offering it, at the time of trial, refer the cause to the inferior judicatory for a new trial; or with the consent of parties take the testimony and issue the case. When, however, this new testimony has had considerable influence in procuring a reversal of the deci-

sion of the court below, this fact shall be distinctly stated in the decision of the superior judicatory.

CHAPTER VIII.

OF SENTENCES.

SECTION 1. A sentence consists in the determination of the degree of censure which is called for, on the finding of charges against an individual true.

2. Sentences should always be as nearly as possible proportioned to the nature and aggravation of the offence, Tit. iii. 10, 11, and adapted to the end. 1 Cor. v. 5; 2 Cor. ii. 6; Jude 22, 23. And if the libel or complaint contained different charges, the sentence must be founded only on such as are duly proved.

3. The sentence, when passed, should be reduced to writing, and read to the party on whom it has been passed. He shall then be required to signify his willingness to submit to it; which if he do, the way is open for its execution. But if he is not prepared to submit, it rests with the judicatory to determine whether, in the circumstances of the case, it will be for edification to grant him time for reflection till the next meeting.

CHAPTER IX.

OF CHURCH CENSURES.

SECTION 1. The censures of the church are

purely spiritual in their character. Having been appointed by the Lord Jesus Christ, to promote the spiritual welfare of his church and people, and He having promised to bind in heaven whatsoever his servants bind on earth, censures administered according to His word cannot be despised or disregarded by men, without guilt and danger: and great solemnity and gravity should be observed by those who administer them, as acting in the name of the great Head of the church.

2. There are five degrees of church censure, namely, admonition, rebuke, suspension, deposition and excommunication.

ARTICLE I.

OF ADMONITION.

Judicial admonition is the lowest degree of censure. It consists in gently reproving an offender for his sin and scandal; warning him of his guilt and danger, and exhorting him to be more circumspect and watchful in the future. It is to be administered in private.

ARTICLE II.

OF REBUKE.

Rebuke is a higher degree of censure, and consists in setting forth the great and aggravated character of the offence, with a sharp reproof for it. Tit. i. 13; ii. 15. Where the offence is private the rebuke should always be in private, and in all cases where the public interests of religion will not be injured thereby, it should be in private. But where the scandal is public, and the sin of an aggravated nature, the censure should be pronounced in public. 1 Tim. v. 20.

ARTICLE III.

OF SUSPENSION.

SECTION 1. Suspension is a censure which may be inflicted on either a private member or an officer of the church. In respect to the former it is a temporary judicial exclusion of an offender from sealing ordinances,* and of the latter, from the exercise of office,† and in ordinary cases from sealing ordinances also.

2. This censure becomes necessary when very gross offences have been committed, or when, notwithstanding admonition or rebuke, an offence is repeated or persisted in, or when probation is necessary to attest repentance and reformation.

3. Suspension may be for a definite time, but generally it must be indefinite in duration, and its removal depend upon the evidence of repentance.

4. Suspension should be public, and may

* See Appendix, No. XV. † See Appendix, No. XVI.

be administered in the absence of the offender.

ARTICLE IV.

OF DEPOSITION.

SECTION 1. Deposition is a sentence depriving a church officer of his office. Ezek. xliv. 13; 1 Kings ii. 27.

2. This censure should not be inflicted but with the greatest deliberation, and for the most weighty reasons, or when lighter censures have failed. It should be preceded by suspension. In the case of ministers, where practicable, the presbytery should seek the advice of synod, and in the case of ruling elders the session should seek the advice of the presbytery, before proceeding to it. The sentence of deposition, passed on a minister, should be publicly intimated in all the congregations of the presbytery, and his congregation declared vacant as soon as possible.

ARTICLE V.

OF EXCOMMUNICATION.

SECTION 1. Excommunication is the judicial excision of an offender from the visible church.* It does not cut him off from the kingdom of grace, but declares him unworthy of a place in the visible church, and to have

* See Appendix, No. XVII.

no more communion with it than "a heathen man and publican." Matt. xviii. 17; 1 Cor. v. 5.

2. This fearful sentence should not be passed except for such gross errors as unhinge the Christian profession, or such violations of the law of God as are peculiarly flagrant, or for obstinate persevering impenitence in grave offences. 1 Tim. i. 13, 20; Matt. xviii. 15—17. And not even then till all Scriptural means have been used, and have failed to reclaim the offender. Matt. xviii. 15—17.

3. Much and solemn deliberation should be exercised before the judicatory proceed to this censure. The session, if they judge themselves shut up to this step, shall refer the matter to the presbytery, who may pass the sentence, if satisfied of its necessity, and give directions for its execution. A presbytery also before excommunicating a minister should consult the synod.

4. In every case before this step is taken, due notice must be given to the offender, and he warned of the sentence which awaits him, unless prevented by speedy repentance. He having been duly notified to attend, the sentence may be passed by the judicatory whether he be present or absent.

5. A warrant having been issued by the presbytery,* for the public intimation of the

* See Appendix, No. XIX.

sentence, the officiating minister, after reading the warrant, shall recount the steps which have been taken in the case, and explain the necessity to which the church has been reduced, of applying this last remedy; and having prayed for the Lord's blessing on his own ordinance, shall solemnly pronounce it in the name of the Lord Jesus Christ.

6. After intimation of the sentence, the members of the church should be warned that the person cast out is no longer to be viewed as a brother, and warned to have no unnecessary intercourse with him. 1 Cor. v. 11—13. Nevertheless, excommunication does not destroy the bonds of natural and civil relations, nor free from any of their obligations. 1 Cor. v. 10; vii. 10—16.

CHAPTER X.

OF THE RESTORATION OF OFFENDERS.

SECTION 1. The Lord Jesus Christ has given to the officers of his house the power to loose as well as to bind, and has promised that whatever they loose on earth, shall be loosed in heaven. Matt. xvi. 19.

2. No degree of heinousness or aggravation of guilt precludes restoration to church privileges on satisfactory evidence of repentance and reformation.

3. It is not, however, every profession of sorrow for sin, nor every promise of amend-

ment, nor even a partial reformation, that should be judged a satisfactory reason for restoration. But where there is manifested a spirit of humility and meekness, accompanied with a watchfulness and circumspection in life and conversation, especially in respect to the particular sin for which the censure has been inflicted, the judicatory may feel themselves warranted in restoring the offender.*

4. The act of restoration shall be public, if the censure was public, otherwise in private, and by the same court which inflicted the censure, unless otherwise directed by the superior judicatory.

5. An offender desirous of restoration shall make application to the court by which he was censured, or to the next superior judicatory, expressing his desire to be restored to the fellowship of the church, acknowledging his sin, and professing his sorrow for it, and his resolution through grace to study to adorn the doctrine of God our Saviour. This, however, shall not preclude the necessity of his giving satisfaction, public or private, as the case may be.

6. Church officers deposed, should not be restored to office, even on evidence of repentance, until some time after an exemplary, humble and edifying conversation. And while it might be sometimes proper to restore them to church privileges, they ought

* See Appendix, No. XVIII. XX.

not, especially ministers, to be restored to the exercise of their office, until it is obvious that the religious community is prepared to receive them in their official character.

CHAPTER XI.

OF DISSENTS AND PROTESTS.

SECTION 1. A dissent is a formal declaration of disagreement with a decision of the court. Any member of a court who is present and voting, may dissent from proceedings which he regards as contrary to the word of God and the standards of the church, and his dissent shall be entered on the record. By so doing, he saves himself from any censure which may arise from these proceedings. If he choose to give his reasons for dissent, these may be placed either on record or on file for preservation, according to the pleasure of the judicatory.

2. The right of dissenting cannot be claimed by a party in a case, nor by any member of the judicatory who was not present or not taking a part in the proceedings. Dissents must be given immediately after the judgment dissented from is pronounced.

3. A protest is a more solemn and formal declaration of disagreement with a decision of a court, testifying against it as an erroneous or injurious judgment, and must be accompanied with a statement of the reasons

on which it is founded, to be in due time handed in and answered by the judicatory.

4. The right of protest belongs not only to the members of the court, but also to either party in a cause which is the subject of investigation and decision, and intimation thereof must be given immediately after the judgment. But no protest can be admitted, unless a party protesting at the same time appeals, or a member protests with a view to appeal or complain to a higher judicatory.

5. If a protest or dissent be couched in decent and respectful language, and contains no offensive reflections or insinuations on the majority of the court, those who offer it have a right to have it recorded in the minutes.

6. The judicatory should appoint a committee to draw up answers to reasons of protest, which, on being adopted, ought to be inserted in the records. A reply on the part of protesters to the answers to their reasons of protest, shall not be admitted. But if they regard the answers as imputing to them opinions or conduct which they disavow, they may ask leave to take back their reasons, and modify them, so as to render them more clearly expressive of their views. Such alteration may be followed by a corresponding modification of the answers, and here this matter must terminate.

7. The admission of a protest by a court

implies no more than a recognition of the right of the protester to exonerate his conscience, or to have a hearing in a superior judicatory.

8. A protest against a decision of the court of last resort may be entered, with the answers, on the records of the court, but such protest does not justify the protester in disobedience or non-submission.

CHAPTER XII.

OF THE VARIOUS WAYS BY WHICH A CASE MAY BE CARRIED FROM A LOWER TO A HIGHER JUDICATORY.

SECTION 1. As the government of the church is conducted by fallible men, wrong may be done by them. To remedy this in an orderly way, is one great design of superior judicatories. When those who had no concern in the origin of proceedings are brought to review them, and annul or confirm them, as they may see cause, there is as great security against permanent wrong as the present imperfect state admits.

2. Every kind of decision which is formed in any church judicatory, except the highest, is subject to review of a superior judicatory, with the limitation contained in Part I., Chapter IX., Section 4, under the head of the General Assembly, and may be brought before it in one or other of the following ways, viz.: by reference, review and control,

appeal, complaint, or declinature. And the members of the lower judicatory, except in cases of reference, shall lose their right to deliberate and vote in the higher judicatory on that particular matter.

ARTICLE I.

OF REFERENCES.

SECTION 1. A reference is a judicial representation, made by an inferior to a superior judicatory, of a matter not yet decided; which representation should be always in writing.

2. Proper subjects of reference are, cases that are new, that are peculiarly delicate or difficult, the decision of which may establish a precedent of extensive influence, or on which the members of the judicatory are much divided.

3. References are either for advice, or for ultimate trial and decision of the case by the superior judicatory.

4. In the former case, the reference merely suspends the decision of the judicatory making it; in the latter case it totally relinquishes the decision, and submits the whole cause to the judgment of the superior judicatory.

5. Although a reference ought, generally, to procure advice from a superior judicatory, yet that judicatory is not bound to give a final judgment in a case, even when requested so to do; but may remit the whole case, with

or without advice, to the judicatory referring.

6. Notice of reference must be given to parties who may be interested in a cause, and the judicatory making the reference should have all evidence duly prepared and in readiness, that the superior judicatory may be able to hear and issue the case with as little delay as possible.

7. References are generally to be carried to the judicatory immediately superior.

ARTICLE II.

OF REVIEW AND CONTROL.

Section 1. It is the duty of every judicatory above a church session, at stated periods, which should be generally once a year, to review the records of the proceedings of the judicatories immediately below. And if any lower judicatory shall neglect to send up its records for this purpose, the higher judicatory may issue an order to produce them, either immediately or at some particular time.

2. In reviewing the records of an inferior judicatory, it will be necessary to examine, First, whether the proceedings have been lawful and regular: Second, whether they have been equitable, faithful, and prudent: Third, whether they have been correctly recorded.

3. The review may be conducted by a

committee, who shall report at the meeting at which they were appointed. If according to the report of the committee, animadversion or censure appear necessary, the members of the inferior judicatory present shall be heard in defence, and the judgment of the court reviewing shall be entered on their own minutes, and on the book reviewed.

4. It may, however, be that in the review, cases of irregular proceedings may be found so injurious and disreputable as to require the interference of the superior judicatory. In such cases the inferior judicatory may be required to review and correct its proceedings, and to report the correction as soon as practicable. If they refuse to correct their errors they may be proceeded against for their refusal.

5. No judicial decision, however, shall be reversed by the judicatory reviewing, unless it be regularly brought up by appeal or complaint.

6. If the superior judicatory be well advised, by common fame, of neglects and irregularities by the inferior judicatory, of which their records give no intimation, or make but an imperfect exhibition, it is incumbent on them to take cognizance of the same. In such cases where notorious errors or sins are suffered to pass without rebuke, and offenders are permitted to escape proper cen-

sure, or where there are circumstances of great irregularity in their proceedings, of which the records give no notice, they shall cite the inferior judicatory to appear and answer, and if it appears that it is culpable, inflict such censure and give such orders as may be judged necessary to remedy the evils existing.

7. While the court of last resort may on all necessary occasions review its own decisions, it is not expedient for an inferior court to do so, except when directed by a superior, or when they become satisfied that there are grounds for the reversal of the decision to which they previously came.

ARTICLE III.

OF APPEALS.

Section 1. An appeal is the removal of a cause which has been already decided, from an inferior to a superior judicatory. It must be under a protest.

2. Appeals may be made either from a definitive sentence as unjust or mistaken, or from any particular step of the proceedings, on account of irregularity, a refusal of reasonable indulgence to a party on trial, declining to receive important testimony, hurrying to a decision before the testimony is all taken, and a manifestation of prejudice in the case.

3. In judicial cases, the right of appeal belongs only to the party against whom the decision is made. In all other cases, when the action or decision of a judicatory inflicts a wrong upon any party or persons, he or they may appeal, and when the purity of the church or the interests of truth and righteousness are affected injuriously by a decision, any member of the judicatory may appeal.

4. In judicial cases, those who have not submitted to a regular trial are not entitled to appeal.

5. Every appellant is bound to give notice of his appeal to the judicatory before it rises, and to lay the reasons thereof in writing, before them at the time, or within ten days thereafter. In the latter case these reasons shall be lodged with the moderator or clerk. But where members or other persons may, for good reasons, not have been present or not have known of the decision, a reasonable time shall be allowed.

6. Appeals should always be carried, in regular gradation, from an inferior to the next higher judicatory.

7. The appellant shall lodge his appeal, and the reasons of it, with the clerk of the higher judicatory, at the commencement of its meeting, and either party may appear in person or in writing. And it shall always be deemed the duty of the judicatory whose

judgment is appealed from, to send authentic copies of all their records, and of the whole testimony relating to the matter.

8. In taking up an appeal in a judicial case, after ascertaining that the appeal has been regularly conducted, the first step shall be to read all the records in the case from the beginning; second, to hear the parties, the appellant first and then the appellee; third, the members of the court shall be called on to give their views, and then the final vote taken. In all other cases of appeal the order of proceeding shall be the same as in cases of complaint.

9. The decision may be to confirm or reverse the decision of the inferior judicatory, either in whole or in part; or to remit the cause, for the purpose of amending the record, should it appear to be incorrect or defective; or for a new trial.

10. If an appeal be sustained, the judgment of the inferior court is necessarily reversed; but if the appeal is not sustained, the judgment is affirmed. In the former case, the superior judicatory, if they see cause, shall either try the cause themselves, or direct the court below how to proceed and issue it. But in case of an appeal from a decision rejecting an appeal, if the appeal be sustained, the case comes on for trial before the higher ju d icatory.

11. If an appellant manifest a litigious or unchristian spirit in the prosecution of his appeal, he shall be censured according to the degree of his offence.

12. If an appellant, after entering his appeal to a superior judicatory, fail to prosecute it, it shall be considered as abandoned, unless he can make it appear that he was providentially prevented.

13. The operation of an appeal is to suspend all further proceedings on the ground of the sentence appealed from. But if a sentence of suspension or excommunication from church privileges, or of deposition from office, be the sentence appealed from, it shall be in force until the appeal shall be issued.

14. In cases where the admission of an appeal would unnecessarily and injuriously delay process, it is competent for the inferior court to refuse to admit an appeal, and having done so, to proceed with the trial, but in such case a party may protest against the rejection of his appeal, and appeal to the superior judicatory.

ARTICLE IV.

OF COMPLAINTS.

SECTION 1. A cause which has been decided in an inferior court, may also be carried before a superior by complaint.

2. A complaint is a representation made to a superior by any member or members of a minority of an inferior judicatory, or by any other person or persons being members of the church, respecting a decision of an inferior judicatory which has been irregular or unjust.

3. Complaints are proper in all cases of grievance, whether judicial or not, where the party aggrieved declines to appeal, or where the complainants do not possess the right of appeal, or where the right of appeal is tyrannically refused; and in all other cases where the complainant is persuaded that the purity of the church or the interests of truth and righteousness are injuriously affected by the decision of an inferior court. But in judicial cases, a party declining to appeal shall not be allowed to complain.

4 The same regulations must be followed in complaints as in appeals. See Article III., Sec. 5, of this chapter.

5. A complaint brings the whole proceedings of an inferior court under the review of its superior, and all parties are thereby placed at the bar of the superior court.

6. In taking up a complaint, if it appear that the complaint has been regularly conducted, all the records in the case shall be read and the parties heard, after which the court shall proceed to consider and decide the case.

7. If on examination it appear that a complaint is well founded, such finding may not only reverse the decision of the court below, either in whole or in part, but also subject the inferior judicatory to such censure as the case may seem to require.

ARTICLE V.

OF DECLINATURES.

SECTION 1. A declinature is the refusal of a person under process to submit to a trial by a particular judicatory.

2. If a judicatory, before a full investigation, by any judicial act prejudge the cause; if they allow members who are nearly related to the opposing party, or who have themselves been active as parties, or at variance with either of the parties, still to sit and vote in the case after objection made—in such cases a declinature is warrantable, if accompanied with an appeal to the next higher judicatory, to be tried by them.

3. But if a person, in order to evade a process, or without assigning any just reason, or without an appeal to the next higher court, declines the authority of his proper judicatory, such declinature is unwarrantable, and does not stay the process, but the person declining may be censured for contumacy.

4. A lawful declinature may be given before any decision is made. But it does not

quash a process. It only removes it to a higher judicatory, where the same regulations shall be observed in the trial as in the cases of appeal.

CHAPTER XIII.

OF JURISDICTION.

SECTION 1. A member dismissed from one congregation, with a view to his joining another, if he commit an offence previous to his joining the latter, shall be considered under the jurisdiction of the church which dismissed him up to the time of his actual reception by that to which he was dismissed. The process, however, after being commenced may be transferred to the session of the church to which he has been dismissed.

2. A minister, in like manner, shall be considered as under the jurisdiction of the presbytery by which he was dismissed until he actually becomes a member of another.

3. Any offence, however, committed by either a minister or member, between the time of his dismissal and his actually joining another body, but which did not come to light until after he had been received by the latter, shall be under the cognizance of the latter body.

CHAPTER XIV.

LIMITATION OF TIME.

SECTION 1. No certificate of church membership shall be considered as valid testimony of the good standing of the bearer, if it be more than one year old, except in cases where there has been no opportunity of presenting it.

2. Process, in case of scandal, shall commence within one year after the crime has been committed, and scandals that have been known for that time, shall not be made the subjects of process, unless they have recently become flagrant. But where a scandal was committed unknown to the church, though more than a year has transpired before its discovery, process may commence as if the crime had recently become flagrant.

3. Persons who have been tried for an offence and acquitted, or found guilty and censured and restored, cannot be subjected to another trial for the same offence.

Respectfully submitted.

J. G. SMART,
J. T. PRESSLY,
J. T. COOPER,
J. CLOKEY,
Committee.

APPENDIX.

I. Testimonial of Members Leaving a Congregation.

That A. B. is a member, in full communion, in the United Presbyterian congregation of ——, in the county of ——, State of ——, and is hereby dismissed at — own request, is attested this—— day of ——, 18—.

By order of Session, J. N., *Mod.*
A. D., *Clerk.*

II. Testimonial for Members who have been some time absent.

That A. N. was a member in full communion in the United Presbyterian congregation of ——, in the county of ——, State of ——, up to the —— day of ——, when — removed from the bounds thereof, and may, as far as is known to this session, be received into the fellowship of any Church of Christ, is attested this —— day of ——, 18—.

By order of Session J. N., *Mod.*
A. D., *Clerk.*

III. Form of Application for the Moderation of a Call.

The United Presbyterian Church at ——, in the county of ——, and State of ——, under the inspection of the Presbytery of ——, being at present vacant, anxious to obtain the stated administration of the word and ordinances among them, and finding themselves able and willing to support it, assembled at ——, on the —— day of ——, 18—, and agreed to petition, and do hereby most heartily petition, the Presbytery for a moderation of a call, and appoint A. N. and C. D. their commissioners, to represent them in this behalf to the Presbytery, at their next meeting.

By order of the Congregation, E. F., *Moderator.*

Done at ——, the —— day of ——, A. D. 18—.

IV. Form of a Call for a Minister.

We, the elders and other members of the United Presbyterian congregation of ——, in the county of ——, and State of ——, taking into our serious consideration the great loss we suffer through the want of a fixed gospel ministry among us, and being fully satisfied, from opportunities of enjoying your public ministrations, that the great Head of the church has bestowed upon you, Mr. A. N., such ministerial gifts and endowments, as, through the divine blessing, may be profitable for our edification: we, therefore, hereby call and beseech you, to come to us and help us, by taking the charge and oversight of this congregation, to labour in it and watch over it, as our fixed pastor: and on your acceptance of this our call, we promise you all due support, respect, encouragement and obedience in the Lord.

In testimony whereof, we have subscribed this our call, this —— day of ——, in the year of our Lord 18—, before these witnesses.

Attest. C. D.
E. F.

V. Attestation of a Call.

That agreeably to presbyterial appointment, I preached on the —— day of ——, in the congregation of ——, under the inspection of the Presbytery of ——, in the State of ——, and presided in the moderation of a call for a pastor to said congregation, which was made out for Mr.

A. N., under the inspection of the Presbytery of ——, is certified at ——, this —— day of ——, A. D. 18—, by

C. D.

VI. Form of an Act of Licensure.

The United Presbyterian Presbytery of ——, in the State of ——, having taken Mr. A. N., student of divinity, on trials for license, and he having acquitted himself to their satisfaction, in all the parts of his trials, did at their meeting on the —— day of ——, at ——, in the county of ——, and State of ——; and hereby do, in the name of the Lord Jesus Christ, allow and appoint him, the said A. N., to preach the gospel of peace within their bounds, and in all other places where in Providence he may be called.

By order of Presbytery, C. D., *Mod.*
E. F., *Clerk.*

Given at ——, county of ——, and State of ——, this —— day of ——, A. D. 18—.

VII. Form of an Edict.

The United Presbyterian Presbytery of ——, in the State of ——, having received a regular call from the congregation at ——, in the —— of ——, and State of ——, to Mr. A. N., preacher of the gospel, to be their minister; and the said Mr. A. N., having undergone trials for ordination; and the Presbytery judging him qualified for the ministry of the gospel, and fit to be pastor of this congregation, the call whereof has been by him accepted, have resolved to proceed to his ordination on the —— day of ——, unless somewhat occur which may lawfully impede it; and, therefore, do hereby give notice to all concerned, that if they, or any of them, have aught to object, why the said Mr. A. N. should not be admitted pastor of this congregation, they may repair to the Presbytery, which is to meet at ——, on the —— day of ——, with certification, that if no objection be then made, the Presbytery will proceed without farther delay.

By order of the Presbytery, C.D., *Mod.*
E. F., *Clerk.*

VIII. Certificate of Ordination.

The United Presbyterian Presbytery of ——, in the State of ——, having had a call from the congregation of ——, county of ——, and State of ——, to Mr. A. N., preacher of the gospel, presented to them, which they sustained, and which he accepted, took him on trials for ordination, and having judged him duly qualified for the office of the gospel ministry, and in particular for the pastoral charge of said congregation; and being presbyterially met at their ordinary place of public worship, on the —— day of ——, did then and there solemnly set apart said Mr. A. N. in the face of the whole congregation there present, to the office of the holy ministry in said congregation, and did afterwards receive him into ministerial fellowship.*

By order of Presbytery, C. D., *Mod.*
E. F., *Clerk.*

Given at ——, on the —— day of ——, A. D. 18—.

IX. Form of Transfer, in Case of a Call from one Presbytery to another.

The United Presbytery of ——, in the State of ——, having received from the Presbytery of ——, in the State of ——, a call for Mr. A. N., to the pastoral charge of the congregation at ——, under the inspection of the Presbytery aforesaid, and said call being by them approved, and by him accepted; they did, and hereby do, transfer and remit him to the Presbytery of ——, for ordination (*or admission*) to the pastoral charge of said congregation.

By order of Presbytery, C. D., *Mod.*
E. F., *Clerk.*

Done at ——, on the —— day of ——, 18—.

* When a candidate is ordained to the ministry at large, or when the Presbytery cannot meet in the congregation to be settled, the form of the testimonials must be varied accordingly.

X. Form of a Commission to the General Assembly.

It is hereby certified, that the United Presbyterian Presbytery of ——, in the State of ——, at their meeting on the —— day of ——, did, and hereby do, appoint Mr. A. N., minister at ——, Mr. C. D., minister at ——, with Mr. E. F. and Mr. G. H., ruling elders, their commissioners to the next General Assembly of this church, to meet at ——, on the —— day of ——, next ensuing; or when and where it shall happen to meet; enjoining them to repair thither, and attend at all the sittings thereof; and there to consult, vote, and determine in all matters that come before them, according to the word of God and the standards of this church, as they will be answerable: and that they report their diligence herein at their return.

By order of Presbytery, J. K., *Mod.*
L. M., *Clerk.*

Done at ——, this —— day of ——, 18—.

XI. Form of a Libel.

Libel preferred against A. N., by order of ——.

Whereas, (here insert the crime) is a heinous sin and scandal, contrary to the word of God, (insert passages) and to the profession of this church, (quote from standards) and injurious to the religion of Christ, and ought to be censured.

Yet true it is that you, A. N., &c., are guilty in the matter of scandal above specified, in so far as you, said A. N. did at —— on the —— day of ——, or thereabouts, (here insert facts) being found relevant and proved against you, you ought to be proceeded against by the censures of the Lord's house, according to the nature of your said offence and scandal.

Signed, E. F., *Mod.*
G. H., *Clerk.*

Done in ——, at ——, this —— day of ——, 18—.

XII. Form of Citation.

By order of the United Presbyterian Session (or Presbytery) of ——, you Mr. A. N., member of, elder or deacon in, or minister at ——, are summoned to appear before said ——, and answer to the libel herewith presented, at ——, on the —— day of ——, and at —— o'clock in the ——.

Signed, C. D., *Mod.*
E. F., *Clerk.*

Done at ——, this —— day of ——, A. D. 18—.

XIII. Form of Citation for a Witness.

Mr. A. N.,

You are hereby summoned by the Session (Presbytery, &c.,) of ——, to appear at ——, on the —— day of ——, to give testimony in a cause pending between C. D. and E. F. Lay aside all excuses and fail not to attend.

A. N., *Mod.*
C. D., *Clerk.*

This —— day of ——, and year of our Lord ——.

XIV. Form of an Oath to be Administered to a Witness.

"You swear by the living God, the searcher of all hearts, that you will declare the truth, the whole truth, and nothing but the truth, according to the best of your knowledge, in the cause now pending, as you shall answer to God at the great day."

XV. Form of an Act of Public Suspension.

Whereas A. N.,* ——hath been convicted before the†

* Member, or elder, or deacon, of this congregation; or minister, elder, deacon, or member of the congregation at ——.

† Session of this church, or Session of the church at ——, or Presbytery of ——.

—— of —— [And whereas the —— have, from time to time, and in the spirit of meekness, endeavoured, without effect, to reclaim their offending brother; *] and whereas his continuing in his sin and refusing to listen to the admonitions of his brethren, render it necessary for the honour of Christ Jesus, for the purity of his religion, for a warning to others, and for his own benefit, to inflict on him a public censure of the Lord's house; the —— did, and hereby do, in the name of the Lord Jesus Christ, and as a court constituted in his name, suspend and exclude the said A. N. from the privileges of the church, till he return from the error of his way, and give solid proofs of unfeigned repentance.

XVI. Form of an Act of Suspension or Deposition from Office.

Whereas A. N. —— hath been convicted before the —— of ——, and whereas it is especially needful, that office-bearers in the house of God be sound in the faith, of good report, and, by their blameless conversation, ensamples to the flock; and whereas the continuance of the said A. N. in the station which he presently holds, is, for these reasons, incompatible with the welfare of the church, the —— aforesaid did, and hereby do, in the name, and by the authority of the Lord Jesus Christ, and according to the powers committed by him unto them as a court constituted in his name,† —— the said A. N. from the office of the ‡ ——, prohibiting him from all and any exercise of the said office of the ‡ —— in the Church of Christ; till he be lawfully restored thereto.

Signed, C. D., *Mod.*
E. F., *Clerk.*

Done in ——, at ——, this —— day of ——.

* The clause included in [——] to be omitted in cases where a public suspension may be necessary without these previous steps.

† Suspend or depose, as the case may require.

‡ Holy ministry, or eldership, or deaconship, according to his station.

The above form is to be observed in those cases where suspension or deposition is necessary, whatever contrition be manifested; but in the event of contumacy, or persisting in the scandal, the following clauses are to be added immediately before the signature of the Moderator and Clerk.

And whereas the said A. B. hath manifested, and doth still manifest contumacious resistance to that authority to which he oweth subjection in the Lord, and refuseth to make just and scriptural satisfaction for his offence; the —— farther did, and hereby do, in the same venerable name, suspend and exclude the said A. B. from the privileges of the Christian Church; with certification, that if he shall not return unto his duty, acknowledging the —— found proved against him, with his contumacious behavior, and confessing his humiliation and penitence therefor, to the glory of God; and apply to the —— against* —— for giving satisfaction with respect to the whole of this his sinful course and conduct, the —— will then consider on proceeding against him by some higher censure, as they shall see cause.

XVII. Form of a Sentence of Excommunication.

Whereas† —— heinous sin and scandal —— proved, at the meeting of the United Presbyterian —— of —— on —— day of —— against Mr. A. B., and whereas the Lord Jesus hath especially given it in charge to the Judicatories of his house, not to suffer sin upon a brother, but, in the fear of God, to endeavor to reclaim him by authoritatively admonishing, rebuking, and otherwise censuring him: all which hath accordingly been done—and whereas he remaineth obstinate and contumacious, without any evidence or sign of repentance, or sorrow for his said scandal and offence, notwithstanding all the reclaiming means which have hitherto been used with him: therefore the —— did, and hereby do, in the name and by the authority of the Lord Jesus Christ, the only king and head of the church, and according to the powers committed by him to them, as a court constituted in his name, actually excommunicate the said A. B., casting him out of the communion of the church of Christ, declaring him to be of those whom the Lord Christ commandeth to be holden by all and every one of the faithful, as heathen men and publicans; and delivering him

* Here insert the time, &c., of satisfaction.
† Matter of, —— or several matters of ——, as the case may be.

unto Satan for the destruction of the flesh, that the spirit may be saved in the day of the Lord Jesus.

C. D., *Moderator*. E. F., *Clerk*.

Done in ——, this —— day of ——.

XVIII. Form of an Act of Absolution and Restoration, as it is to be intimated to one who has been Excommunicated.

Whereas thou, A. B., hast, for thy sin, been shut out from the communion of the faithful, and hast now manifested thy repentance, wherein the church resteth satisfied: the —— in the name, and by the authority of the Lord Jesus Christ, and according to the powers committed by him to them, as a court constituted in his name, did, and hereby do, absolve thee from the censure of excommunication formerly pronounced against thee, and do restore thee to the communion of the church, and the free use of all the ordinances of Christ, that thou mayst partake of all his benefits to thy eternal salvation.

XIX. Form of a Presbyterial Warrant for intimating the Censure on Excommunication.

The —— of —— having found just cause of excommunication against A. B. on account of —— and of aggravated contumacy and impenitence therein, and having, at their meeting at —— on the —— day of —— excommunicated him accordingly; did, and hereby do appoint you, Mr. C. D., minister of the gospel at —— to intimate said censure to the congregation at —— on —— day, the —— day of —— in the ordinary place of public worship, and immediately after the conclusion of the —— service, and in the following words: (Here insert the act of excommunication.)

:X. Form of a Presbyterial Warrant for intimating the Absolution and Restoration of a Penitent.

The —— of —— having found just and sufficient cause of absolving A. B. from the censure of excommunication under which he presently lies, and of restoring him to the priviliges of the Lord's house; and having, at their meeting at —— on the —— day of —— absolved and restored —— accordingly, did, and hereby do appoint and direct you, Mr. C. D., minister of the gospel at —— to intimate —— absolution and restoration to the congregation at —— on —— day of —— in the ordinary place of public worship, and immediately after the conclusion of the —— service, and in the words following: (Here insert the act of absolution.)